Men and Their Work

Men and Their Work

by Everett Cherrington Hughes

GREENWOOD PRESS, PUBLISHERS
WESTPORT, CONNECTICUT

6936

Library of Congress Cataloging in Publication Data

Hughes, Everett Cherrington, 1897-
    Men and their work.

    Reprint of the ed. published by Free Press, Glencoe,
Ill.
    Bibliography: p.
    Includes index.
    1. Occupations. 2. Social classes. I. Title.
[HT675.H8 1981]   306'.3   80-29143
ISBN 0-313-22791-8 (lib. bdg.)

Reprinted in 1981 by Greenwood Press
A division of Congressional Information Service, Inc.
88 Post Road West, Westport, Connecticut 06881

Printed in the United States of America

10 9 8 7 6 5 4 3 2 1

TO
My Two Helens
AND
My Two Elsies

Contents

Preface

A MAN'S WORK is as good a clue as any to the course of his life, and to his social being and identity. This has been so longer than we sociologists, with our love of stereotypes of the past against which to highlight the present, allow. The new thing is that the number of kinds of work to be done is so great as to be confusing to the young person trying and, indeed, compelled to get into one. The changes wrought in known and historic occupations by new technology, new organization and by social movements within a man's life-time—or more exactly, within his work-time—make the confusion worse confounded. One may find himself earning his living at work that neither he nor those who guided him (teachers, parents and knowing peers) had heard of when he was in school. He may find that the cherished object of his and his parents' ambition and hard work is "automated" to splinters; or that the profession which was to make him free nowadays makes him a cog in a great machine.

Many new and some old occupations have sought for themselves the envied status of *profession;* some of them succeed in gaining that esteem, that broad license to control their work and that social mandate over affairs pertaining to it that the term *profession* connotes. A man may get into a dying trade, an old one being transformed in its essential aspects, a new one on the way up, or even a new one already falling short of the aspirations of its still living founders and advocates. The resulting problems of the definition and control of occupations and of careers of individuals are many. Hence, although a man's work may indeed be a good clue to his personal and social fate, it is a clue that leads us— and the individual himself—not by a clear and single track to a known goal, but into a maze full of dead-ends and of unexpected adventures.

Of course not all, or even any great proportion, of people are confused unduly by the world of work, either in advance or as they get on into it. The bureaucratic trend has so penetrated business and industry that more and more people have assurance, at least on paper, of a smooth and well-marked march by easy stages from the high-school guidance office to a retirement suitable to one's achievements. Some of the best sociological research of recent years has had to do with the great bureaucratic organizations in which much of the work of our economy is done. One thinks of the fruitful hypotheses and findings concerning human groups which have emerged from study of what is commonly, though badly, called "restriction of production." But the trend towards large organizations and toward the bureaucratizing of careers does not do away with the struggle of the individual to find a place and an identity in the world of work or with the collective efforts of occupations to exert control over the terms of their work with and for others.

It is with these latter problems that the papers in this volume are concerned; with the social psychological, rather than with the organizational aspects of work; and with the professional and would-be professional rather than with the industrial and bureaucratic occupations. This is so, not by design (although I have left out some papers on industrial problems), but by the accident—if it be one—of the bent of my own work. Yet I think it can fairly be said of the papers that they clearly imply, where they do not state, that the *career of a man* is worked out in some organized system without reference to which it cannot be described, much less understood; and that the *career of an occupation* consists of changes of its internal organization and of its place in the division of labor of which society itself consists.

The papers do not so much report the details of research as discuss ideas which grew out of whatever study or series of studies I was working on at the time. The late Professor Robert E. Park asked me, then a graduate student, to write a paper on my not yet finished study of the attempt of real estate men to gain power and the status of a profession; the result was "Personality Types and the Division of Labor." One of the latest, " The Making of a Physician," was a statement designed to get support of a foundation for study of a medical school. The foundation was not impressed, but four of us, myself and colleagues (two of whom were once my students) are in the exciting midst of the study (thanks to support from a more modest quarter).

My debts lie, therefore, in two directions. I was greatly taught and greatly encouraged by Professors Small, Park and Faris and continue to be so by my teacher and colleague, Professor Burgess. But those best of all colleagues, my students, have also encouraged me by their interest; and, bettering their instruction, they continue to teach me. I have exploited their observations and their ideas in these papers, probably even more than I know. May these papers suggest still new and fruitful studies to still other students who will become colleagues.

My apologies are due the reader for not including reference to many recent important articles and books on professional and other kinds of work. The bibliography includes only those things referred to in the original articles here reproduced.

EVERETT CHERRINGTON HUGHES

1

Cycles, Turning Points,
and Careers

EVERY MAN is born, lives, and dies in historic time. As he
runs through the life-cycle characteristic of our species, each
phase of it joins with events in the world. In our society, the
successive phases of his life tend to be defined in terms of his
relations to the world of school and work: pre-school, school,
work, and retirement. But some people come to the age of
work when there is no work; others when there are wars. A
man may learn the trade of, say, furrier; start a small shop
in a solid city neighborhood only to have technological and
economic changes make him and the shop slightly obsolete
and to have his customers desert to the suburbs when he is
too old to learn the new techniques and to raise the new
capital required for a smart suburban shop, yet too young to
retire decently. Such joining of a man's life with events,
large and small, are his unique career, and give him many
of his personal problems.

But not all of a man's life is his work; and not all of it

The main body of this paper was prepared for the Eighth Annual Con-
ference on Theology in Action, Adelynrood, South Byfield, Mass., Septem-
ber, 1950, and was published by the National Council of the Episcopal
Church, as a Faculty Paper, in 1952, with the title *Cycles and Turning
Points*. It is here reprinted with permission.

is unique in the sense of being very different from the courses of other men's lives. There is a certain order in the lives of men in a society. Some of the ordering is open, intentional, and institutionalized; some of it happens without people quite knowing it until it is turned up by investigation. The ordering in our society, as I have mentioned above, is very much a matter of a man's relation to the world of work. It is also true that our institutions of work are highly developed and are, in unusual measure, formally separated from others. There are a time and a place for work; times and places for family life, recreation, religion, and politics. The mood and frame of mind of the place of work are supposed to be different from those of the rest of life. The study of the more or less orderly and predictable course of a man's work life has become a major concern of several branches of academic endeavor. Some of the essays which follow in this volume have to do with careers in just this sense. This essay, however, treats of the phases and turning points of a man's whole life. It is included in a volume of essays on work just because it does see a man's life as a whole, of which his work is but one facet.

Every culture develops a calendar; some cycle of days, moons, positions of sun and stars, or rain and drought, heat and cold, of plenty and want; of germination, growth, and harvest of plant; of breeding, birth, growth and migration of the animals upon which they depend. These cycles of nature are interlaced with man's cycle of work and play and with his movements from place to place. Anthropologists have given us a rich body of descriptions of these cycles among the peoples of the world and of the myriad rites, festivals, exorcisms, and the like which mark their turning points. They tell us of cycles of mood as well as of natural occurrence, of periods of black despair followed by gay renewal of life and hope. A tribe may, with its most powerful rites, compel the sun to stop his flight to the south and to turn northward so as to bring summer again. It may combine abstinence, fasting, and repentance of sin with its most impressive ceremonials to make the rains come after seasonal drought or to make them stop ere the earth dissolve in moisture. We are all aware of the way in which the ancient cycle of solstice and equinox has become woven into the Christian calendar. Whether the rites which accompany the turning of the wheel of time among so many of the peoples of the world are of the essence of religion or not, certainly one cannot say much about religions without taking the calendar of rites into account. And certainly no people has for long lived without some established groupways which turn with the sun.

All cultures also recognize and mark in various ways the biological life-cycle of the human individual. Birth is attended by rites which acknowledge the social existence of the infant, and make him a member of his kin-group and of his community. At the same time, his parents are ritually made into father and mother and assume responsibility for developing and training their offspring into good members of the community. Further rites often occur at puberty, when membership in one sex or the other becomes a more fateful matter; or when a boy is ready to go to sea, to war, or to the hunt with adult males. Entering upon a trade, marrying, growing old, and dying are also celebrated. These are all cases of passage from one status to another, from one patterned combination of duties and privileges, with its attendant perils and joys, to another. After the phrase of van Gennep, they have come to be called *rites de passage,* rites of transition. Sometimes the transition from one status to another is considered of such import that the candidate is given special instructions in the canons of conduct appropriate to his new estate. He may be sent upon a lonely journey in search of a vision, separated from other people and ordinary activities for a time, subjected to severe ordeals and bound by solemn vows. He may be made symbolically to die as a child and to be born again as a man. Finally he may appear again in the world transfigured, in a new costume and like St. Paul, bearing a new name.

Not only is the biological life-cycle of the individual thus related to the corresponding social cycle of his standing in society, but account is also taken of occasional cycles of mood and condition, that is, of the things which, while not so fixed in their order as are birth, puberty, aging and death, are pretty sure to happen to all men, life and human nature being what they are. One may violate a tabu, commit a sin, or do an injury to another. A man may have been ill and in his fever may have seen the spirits of the dead. A woman may be bereft of the man whose bed and board she shared so closely that they were as one life. These things alienate one from other men and women, and from the routine and banality of life. Many societies have institutionalized this alienation. In India the widow jumped into the funeral pyre and joined her husband in death. More commonly, there are rites for bringing the person, in due time, back into the world. In French Canada, a young widow mourns her young husband for a time, starting with the severest of black costume and gradually returning to one which suggests that though she be a woman with a sorrow, her youth, attractiveness, and fruitfulness are not to be wasted. There is a period and a depth of mourning appropriate to every age and state of the mourner and the mourned, and to every degree of kin. In some societies, mourning is brought to an end after a stated period, and in a ceremonial way. The bereaved arises, puts on new garments, and goes among men again.

How well, in each case, does the proper institutional expression suit the felt grief of the bereaved individual? How often is it a hypocritical cover? How often a woefully insufficient expression of deep feeling? How often does the fixed penance for sin really liquidate the sense of guilt? How often is the rite gone through with defiant unrepentance? These are appropriate questions, but one cannot answer them in the mass. I suppose that if the instituted rites no longer correspond fairly well to the cycles and degrees of feeling accompanying the crises they are intended to carry one over, one would have to say that something is out of joint in society; that is, if the psychological reality and the social institution are no longer in some good functioning relation to one another. However that may be, there is one great thing to be said for conventional and instituted rites for carrying people over such crises, and for passing them on from one state of life to another; namely, that so long as the rites are practised there is no attempt to deny the realities of the human life-cycle, and the contingencies and changes of status that occur during it, and there is no pretense that the rhythms of mood, of guilt, of unhappiness and grief do not occur. I am afraid that many of us, in our culture and in our time, do try to deny these things, to exorcise the reality by the negative rite of looking firmly in the opposite direction so as to pretend nothing is happening.

The number of phases of the social life-cycle varies from society to society and may be altered by social changes of many kinds. The passage from one phase to another may be obscured or prolonged. In our society, the ages of entering and leaving school and of going to work and supporting one's self have been undergoing great change. We are far from the simple state of rural Quebec where a boy is a man when, for the first time, he goes to the field and handles a team of horses. On that day, when he comes in to dinner he eats with the men and, before returning to the field, hauls down a pipe from the rack near the kitchen stove and smokes a pipeful of home-grown, home-cured tobacco, even if it nearly kills him. With us, a man's graduation from college or professional school may be attended by his own children. A physician, on the average, does not make ends meet until he is past thirty years of age. It is therefore difficult to say when childhood ceases, when adolescence begins and ends, when one is really adult. The onset and the risks of middle age are altered by technological and social change. The functions of old age are perhaps less clearly defined than ever before, in spite of the fact that there is an increasing tendency to standardize the age of retirement from work and the movement to provide pensions and thus economic security for all people.

As for marriage, the women of our time run a greater risk of having no man at all than have the women of any other civilization; yet they are completely without ritual defences and without clear definitions and rationalizations of their enforced celibacy. It may be the confusion of age lines, the lack of moments of clear-cut change, which makes us a bit unwilling to recognize the turns from one life-phase to another. That we are loathe to recognize many of the crucial turnings is, I think, beyond dispute. And we much dislike to mark one age from another by costume and ornament, or by terms of address and etiquette. And, while the psychiatrist is familiar with the private rituals by which people try to reduce their sense of guilt, we are especially loathe to recognize it socially as something requiring periodic public ceremonial liquidation. And as Margaret Mead has pointed out, we even try to do away with death. The modern hospital, in its anxiety to appear to be a place where all patients get well, refuses to allow relatives to gather for a ceremonial parting from a loved one, and condemns the dying to sanitary solitude. If there be any triumph in death, our generation will not be there to see it. As for mourning, we are so fearful of wearing sorrow upon our sleeves, that we eat our hearts out in a mourning which cannot be brought to a decent end, because it has never had a proper beginning. I have had dear friends who have done it so; and so has anyone who is of that well-meaning generation who believed that all good things could be attained by science and all bad things avoided by emancipation from old formulae and freedom from old distinctions; the people who got it into their heads that anything formal is cold—not sensing that ceremonial may be the cloak that warms the freezing heart, that a formula may be the firm stick upon which the trembling limbs may lean; that it may be a house in which one may decently hide himself until he has the strength and courage to face the world again.

How ghastly can be the smile of a suffering man who is pretending that all is well; how pathetic the stiff but tottering stance of a man who, because he does not know how to share his troubles with others through the historic liturgies, is about to break under them. How pathetic, also, the man who, in his time of trouble, expresses the ultimate of that individualism in which we have all been reared—the insistence that his troubles are so private and so unique that no social salve can soothe them.

The trouble may have been that, since we believed in progress, in things getting better and better, we were—and are—unwilling to face the implication of inevitability that lies in a repeated rite. A rite is something which is set off, so to speak, by a trigger, by something which happens again and again. To observe a rite is a sort of confession that the occasion of it may happen again and again in the future as it has in the past. It is as if the magnitude of progressive changes had blinded us to the limits within which change occurs. The average life-expectancy of the child at birth has increased so marvelously that we overlook the fact that the oldest man alive now is probably no older than the oldest man alive in the days of great Caesar, and no older in medically progressive America than in backward India. Our average health is so good that we forget that man is as mortal as ever. And perversely enough, as the belief in life after death has declined, we have become less and less willing to make an occasion of death itself. Those who have the cure of souls in their charge—pastors, psychiatrists—can tell better than I what burdens break and what sicknesses ravage the souls of people who, in the name of self-reliance, emancipation or progress, try to act as if there were no cycle of youth, maturity, old age, and death; no rhythms of inner peace and conflict, of guilt and freedom from guilt, of grief and of the healing of its wounds.

I began with some statements concerning the calendar and went from that to the problem of the life cycle of the individual. Let us return to the calendar, for the two are closely related. Revolutionary movements are invariably enemies of the existing calendar for the very good reason that the calendar embodies the social memory. Every day is rich with meaning; the more festive days and seasons blow into flame the cooling embers of sentiment. The calendar is the warp of the fabric of society, running lengthwise through time, and carrying and preserving the woof, which is the structure of relations among men, and the things we call institutions.

The men of the French revolution tried to cut off the warp of memory by changing the names of days and even months; they went further, and tried to break the rhythm of life itself by changing the number of days in the weeks and of months in the years. This is a logical thing for men to do when they want to change society completely. Its relation to rites is obvious.

Sectarian movements, bent upon religious revolution, likewise attack the calendar. Insofar as purification of an ancient religion is their aim, they see in the calendar and the rites that are timed by it, the barnacles of corrupt tradition which have gathered upon the strong, clean hull of doctrine and practice. But there is another logic behind the sectarian attack. It is hinted at in Dom Gregory Dix's *Shape of the Liturgy*, in a magnificent chapter entitled, "The Sanctification of Time." The early Christians developed little in the way of a calendar in the centuries before Constantine. Why? Because they were a little band of faithful people holding themselves in constant readiness for the end of the old and the beginning of the new.

They did not look back. Since the danger of death and damnation and the hope of Christ's coming were equal in all moments of time (*Ye know not the day nor the hour*), one had to be equally in a state of grace at all times. Hence, one day could be no more dedicated to the service of God than another. As time went on, the Christians made some peace with the world; as generations turned, they began to accumulate memories, to take account of rhythms and cycles, to recognize that some among the saints are more constant than others and that the best of us have our ups and downs. So they developed devices for meeting the recurrent smaller crises of life while waiting for the great final crisis. Thus it is with the recurring revivals and movements for the purification of religion. Some man, himself at white heat, conceives of a church of people all at constant white heat. Only those who are aware of their lost condition and who have consciously repented and believed, only those whose devotion is full and complete, are members of the true church. You will see this ideal described in John Locke's famous *Letters concerning Toleration*. It was embodied in the Quaker meeting in its early form.

Since it could not be allowed that devotion could or should vary from moment to moment, or from day to day, there could be no holy days, no cycles, no calendar. Thus Edmund Gosse in *Father and Son* tells how his father, Philip Henry Gosse, threw into the garbage-can the Christmas pudding which a sympathetic cook had secretly prepared for the small boy. The father was of the Brethren who did not approve of special Christian days and especially hated joyous festivity in the name of religion. The ceremonies of renewal imply that faith and fervor cool and want reheating. That the true sectarian zealot cannot allow.

Likewise, since entering the Church is purely a matter of reasonable conviction, it must be a single, catastrophic act of a person of the age called that of discretion. Hence that horror of infant baptism so common among strict sectarian groups. Edmund Gosse, again, reports his childish wondering about what terrifying sinful practice lay behind the mysterious epithet, *paedo-baptist*—the anxious fear that something less than unwavering white heat of fervor is inimical to the cycles of growth and changes of state implied in a series of rites of religious initiation and transition beginning in infancy or childhood.

Now these features of early Christian and of sectarian mentality generally are of more than historical interest. For the sectarian revolt against calendars and cycles is something that occurs again and again. And as often as it occurs, the facts of life slowly or rapidly catch up with the revolting group. For one thing, even sectarians have children. In theory, these offspring of the saints may be outside the Church until they are violently converted at some age called that of discretion. But people are not really that hard-hearted when they become parents. Besides, conversion in course of time tends to come and to be expected to come at a certain age, usually adolescence. A Baptist student told me how, when he was fourteen, his parents and the pastor openly expected him to be soundly converted between Christmas and that time in the spring when the water would be warm enough for an open-air baptizing in New Brunswick. His age-mates, who were with him in a special class for the purpose, saw the light one after another. He alone got no sign from heaven. He got to feeling so guilty that he finally felt compelled to testify to an experience which he had not had. The words came easily from the formulae in which he had heard others tell what they had felt in conversion. Then for weeks, while he basked in the sunlight of general approval during the day, he lay awake at night fearing that his lie was the unpardonable sin. James Weldon Johnson tells a similar story of his Negro Methodist youth in Florida. He, too, lied, but in verse and made a career of it.

One could go on with examples of the growth of calendars. The early Methodist camp-meeting and revival were outbreakings of the spirit, whenever and wherever it might please God; but in due time God pleased more and more often to have the camp meeting right after harvest when a joyous spirit coincided with a slack in the farm work, and to have the revival in the dead of winter when life was dark and dreary. Gradually the revival has merged back into Holy Week. The shoutings of the Negro meeting have settled into rhythms and chants.

The single-minded logic of hard reason, of unwavering devotion, of equal sanctity of the days, gives way to the rhythms and cycles of birth, growth, and decline and death. The fanatical insistence that all men be equally strong and constant gives way to a measure of charity for the young and the weak, and to devices to bring both weak and strong back into grace after a fall. It is, I suppose, the dialectic of time and eternity, of the absolute unchanging ideal and of the relative changing reality.

The manner in which any society or epoch handles this dialectic is one of its distinguishing marks, and is one of the things which will, I am convinced, determine the kinds of soul sickness from which its members will suffer.

As for our own times, William Graham Sumner said of us even half a century ago that we no longer like to take vows; that is, to make commitments for ourselves. He might have added that, in the name of emancipation and of respect for the individual, we do not like to make commitments for others, even for our own children. And in all rites of initiation or transition there is commitment either for one's self or for someone else, or for both. I even know a woman who did not want to name her children more than tentatively so as to leave them the freedom to pick their own names to suit whatever notions they might get of themselves. She could not bear being a *paedonomist,* I suppose. When and if it becomes possible to control the sex of unborn children, we will no doubt breed a generation of hermaphrodites for fear of committing our children to an identity and a fate not of their choosing.

I wonder what is back of all this. Perhaps it is that sectarian Protestantism has lost the individual faith and fervor which allowed several magnificent generations of rugged individualists to do without a calendar, and without the support, direction and comfort of liturgy and rites of passage. Without their faith, but with a scruple for the feelings of others, and especially of our own offspring, that our immediate predecessors lacked, we are unwilling to commit ourselves and even more unwilling to commit our children to anything, even to a social identity. And in so doing, we rob them of the ultimate inalienable right of every child: a good and sound reason for running away from home. That is the last indignity which the child-centered home heaps upon its miserable victims.

2

Personality Types
and The Division of Labor

THIS ESSAY does not have to do with personality types in the terms of the many tests devised by psychologists for revealing subtle and deep-lying as well as gross and obvious differences among individuals. Indeed, I doubt whether I would give this title to the paper if I were writing on the same problems now. I would not, however, give up the use of the term personality to refer to what the human being becomes when he gains status, not merely by being assigned to some of the major differentiating categories of the society in which he lives, but by acquiring a place in a series of sub-groups with variant versions and refinements of the attitudes and values of the prevailing culture. The division of labor provides many such sub-groups in which a man may live and have his being. If, as W. I. Thomas said, personality is the subjective aspect of culture, then a man's work, to the extent that it provides him a subculture and an identity, becomes an aspect of his personality.

The paper was written just as I had finished and was about to submit as a Ph. D. thesis, a study of the Chicago Real Estate Board. One might say that it rides madly off in

The American Journal of Sociology, Vol. XXXIII (March, 1928), 754-768. Reprinted with modifications, by permission.

all directions from that study, chasing one problem after another a little way.

Literature and common sense, and, in these latter days, the press, have given us stereotyped pictures of persons engaged in various occupations: the old-maid school teacher, the parson, the village blacksmith, the farmer, the professor, the politician, the financier. All these and many other types so created are expected to react to the situations of life in characteristic manner. To many the cartoonist adds a face and costume. Social scientists and philosophers have taken the cue and have sometimes related types of men to their tasks, as Adam Smith in his classic paragraph on the nature of the differences between the philosopher and the man with a wheelbarrow. In common-sense discussion the question is not asked as to the manner in which the differences arise: it only talks of them as facts or fiction.

In our branch of social science much attention has lately been turned to the classification of persons into types, according to their behavior. Some of the older classifications, as good and bad, criminal and and law-abiding, rich and poor, have been called into question—not because the classes indicated do not exist, but because they do not give sufficient clues to the behavior of people. Professor Ernest W. Burgess has undertaken to study the delinquent as a person, taking into account sequences of behavior, the rôles assumed by the person in his group, the rôle accorded him by his group; and with the further provision that one take into account the group in which the person wishes to have status. That is to say, the group in which he "lives." The delinquency, or the breaking of the law, thus becomes a mere item in a pattern of behavior, and emphasis is put on the fact that this one item is not always the same, even when the overt act involved comes under a given legal category. In this is a recognition that behavior types do not necessarily coincide with the common-sense or legal definitions.

In this paper we appear to be reverting from the position already gained; looking for a set of personality types in a classification of people according to the work they do. A number of questions at once arise. To what extent do persons of a given occupation "live together" and develop a culture which has its subjective aspect in the personality? Do persons find an area for the satisfaction of their wishes in the associations which they have with their colleagues, competitors, and fellow-servants? To whose opinions is one sensitive? What part does one's occupation play in giving him his "life-organization"?[1]

A prerequisite for the answering of these questions is study of persons engaged in various occupations, to determine the nature of occupational selection, and what happens to a person once he does find a place in the division of labor. A number of such studies have been undertaken. Some are statistical studies; others are what one might call case studies of occupations, as Mrs. Donovan's work on the waitress.[2] We can go no farther in this paper than to put the problem into a frame of reference, and illustrate from one occupational group.

HUMAN ECOLOGY AND
THE DIVISION OF LABOR

We are indebted to Durkheim for a distinction between two types of social units, the *social segment* and the *social organ*. The *social segment* is that sort of minute community which exists in independence of all others; its members grow up under conditions so uniform that their consciences are concrete, uniform, and strong. It is also characterized by the

---

1. Thomas, W. I., and Znaniecki, F. *The Polish Peasant in Europe and America* (New York, A. A. Knopf, 1927) 2d ed.; Vol. I, p. 27.
2. Donovan, Frances R. *The Woman Who Waits,* Boston, 1920.

presence of as many generations as the longevity of the group allows. It is different in a number of ways from all other communities. The individual cannot imagine any other set of social attitudes than the one common to the people of his own group. The *social organ,* on the other hand, is dependent for life upon other communities; it represents only a unit in the division of labor, and must engage in exchange with other communities. This exchange requires at least a minimum of understanding between the groups of communities involved. The division of labor represents a set of exchanges between communities whereby these communities become involved as functioning parts of a larger community. This larger community, however, has no common conscience, or only a very tenuous, vague, abstract one. As the division of labor proceeds, the life of each social organ is more conditioned by the others; the forces which hold it in place come to include neighbors as well as the soil beneath one's feet. It is this pattern of social organs, treated spatially, with which human ecology concerns itself.

SACRED DIVISION OF LABOR

In the type of community which Durkheim calls a "social segment" the division of labor is either very simple or very rigid. It may be mere incident of the social organization of the community, consisting in sets of sacred prerogatives, as in the caste system, where a person is born to his trade and station. We may call this sort of division of labor a sacred one. The prerogatives of a given caste may or may not constitute a unit of technique.

In a study of the division of labor among preliterates, done under the tutelage of Professor Ellsworth Faris at the University of Chicago, the writer isolated a set of occupations which he called "preliterate professions," including healers, performers of rituals, charmers, medicine men, etc. In them he found associated with a certain amount of practical technique a great amount of secret ritual and prerogative whose connections with each other were traditional and arbitrary and fortified by taboos. In a society where the division of labor is of this character, its relation to personality is fairly obvious, especially if it include the "caste" feature of evaluation and a complete set of social relationships involved with it. This type of division of labor is essentially a phenomenon of an unchanging, immobile society. There may be a tendency for it to develop in a changing society, or at least to persist. For instance, one can think of no principle of technique which naturally associates the activities of the clergyman: he directs the business affairs of his parish, marries, baptizes, comforts the sad, prays for the recovery of the sick, and acts as interpreter of morals and theology. The functions are set in a traditional and somewhat arbitrary complex; they are prerogatives.

As Cecil North puts it:

"A group in which status, occupation, and culture have become hereditary is known as a caste. As a matter of fact, however, the distinction between a society based upon caste and one in which open classes prevail is simply one of degree. There are present in all societies forces which tend to crystallize the form of social institutions and social organization. And it is merely a question of how freely these forces have made themselves or worked themselves out to a logical conclusion."[3]

THE SECULARIZATION OF
THE DIVISION OF LABOR

In contrast to this type we may characterize the division of labor in our world as secularized. New occupations are created every day, and the concatenations of functions of old

---

3. North, C. C. *Social Differentiation*. Chapel Hill, 1926, p. 255.

ones are subject to change. The industrial revolutions of every day mean to the individual that he is not sure of his job; or, at least, that one is not sure of one's son's job. This is true of whole regions, as well as of individuals; changes in transportation, methods of production, extension of the frontiers of commerce do violence to the most deeply rooted and sacred prerogatives.

Again North has put the point well:

> "The discovery of new territory or natural resources, the appearance of new inventions or new fields of industry, the coming of war—all tend to upset the old arrangement and make for an exchange of places on the social ladder. A high state of intelligence and communication will make it possible for individuals to pass up or down in the scale according to their abilities and character."[4]

Occupational selection becomes a major process, to which social organization is incidental. This selection becomes a fierce process which begins anew each day, atomizing families and tearing them loose from their soil.

We may call the division of labor "secularized" both in that new occupations or units of function are developed, which are not hampered by tradition, and in that the persons who enter the occupation come without very definite, traditional notions about the way of carrying on the occupation.[5] We shall pursue this point further in consideration of what the occupational selection process is and what it does to the person.

OCCUPATIONAL SELECTION

In his recent work, *Wirtchaftsleben im Zeitalter des*

---

4. *Ibid.*

5. Sombart, Werner. *Das Wirtschaftsleben im Zeitalter des Hochkapitalismus* (Munich, Duncker & Humblot, 1927). Erster Halbband, p. 30. Sombart states that "the secularization of the capitalistic spirit must be regarded as one of the most important developments of modern times." It lets anyone try anything.

Hochkapitalismus,[6] Sombart has made his major theme the selection of the leaders of industry, as well as that of the proletariat. The chief point in regard to the former is that the life-histories of a very large percentage of them show small beginnings. The corporation and the credit system have made this possible. This fact of democratization does not mean an increase in the chances of the person of low degree to rise in the economic and social scale so much as an acceleration of change, the disappearance of old occupations, and the rise of new ones. Sombart makes this clear in his consideration of the sources of the proletariat. The proletariat comes from the ranks of those, says he, who have been dislodged from their traditional places on the soil, and from those whose birth and family do not presume for them any place in the economic system except a place which the individual himself may find. Selection of occupations of the proletarian sort depends largely on time and place availability, both of the job and the person who fills it. North concludes[7] that "the determination of the precise task that most individuals perform within the larger class of occupations lies in chiefly local, temporary, and fortuitous circumstances." The sum total of conclusions from most of contemporary discussion is that one can predict neither the occupational fate of the individual nor the origin of the person who will next fill a given job. It amounts to a recognition of the essentially complicated nature of the processes involved.

In certain types of occupations the process can be analyzed within certain limits; as, for instance, in the clergy of evangelical churches where one needs a more definite "call" to the profession. This call comes more frequently to rural youths than to urban. The country furnishes the ministers for the city. Also the more evangelical churches furnish the ministers for the less evangelical. The Unitarian denomination

---

6. *Ibid.,* p. 19.
7. *Op. cit.,* p. 235.

furnishes practically no ministers, but must recruit its prophets from emancipated ones of more orthodox denominations. The occupation of the parent undoubtedly has certain tendencies to affect that of the children. The minister's son, for example, has a flair for more emancipated occupations, but still retains some of the father's tendency to appraise rather than participate in the life of the community. Sociology is full of ministers' sons. These processes of selection may well be studied both by case studies of occupations and of families.

THE DIVISION OF LABOR AND
THE MOBILITY OF THE PERSON

The secularized division of labor is a most powerful mobilizer of persons. Durkheim stated this fact as one of the first order of importance among the effects of an increased division of labor upon social life.

> "For to live by a métier one must have clients, and he must sally forth from his house to find them; he must sally forth also to enter into relations with his competitors, to struggle against them, and to converse with them. Moreover, métiers suppose more or less directly, cities, and cities are always formed and recruited principally by means of immigrants who have quitted their *milieu natal*."[8]

The persons who become commodities or functionaries in the division of labor have been reared in families. In the family the person has acquired a set of social objects and attitudes more or less common to the community. To get into the occupational world, one must be mobilized. This mobilization, according to its degree, implies a removal from

8. Durkheim, Emile. *De la division du travail social.* Préface à la deuxième édition. "Quelques remarques sur les groupements professionelles." (Paris: F. Alcan, 1902.) Translation of this passage by ECH.

See subsequently published translation by George Simpson: *The Division of Labor in Society.* 1933, and 1947.

the base of one's morals. The study of *The Polish Peasant in Europe and America* (Thomas and Znaniecki) shows nothing more clearly than that this removal ends in radical personality changes. Eugenia Remmelin, in her unpublished study of *Itinerants,* suggested that the itinerant is, by his very itineracy, cut off from the more settled world over which he moves. These two examples represent, respectively, an extreme of initial movement and an extreme in degree of mobility in a given type of occupation. The essential fact of the mobilizing of the person for participation in economic life is only less, not different, in character in other and more common cases. The process of finding a place in competition with others is one involving a great deal of spatial movement in a world where urbanization is proceeding at a rapid rate. Professor Sorokin gives us statistics to show that in 1920 one-third of the people of the United States lived outside the states in which they were born. He assumed that the number living outside the communities in which they were born would be much higher.[9]

The general circulation of population over the face of the earth is continually putting individuals in countries whose language they do not know, and in whose social scheme they have no place. The effect of this mobilization on existing social groups is called, by students of family disorganization, atomizing of the family. Perhaps it does not completely atomize the family, but at least it breaks larger kin connections into smaller clusters of people who have attained about the same occupational levels and styles of life.

The Catholic clergy probably represents the most complete removal of the person from his *milieu natal* for professional life. In a West Side community in Chicago the writer became acquainted with a number of Irish families who had sons in a seminary. In each case the attitude of the family was one of conflict between pride at the son's achievement

---

9. Sorokin, P. *Social Mobility* (New York: Harper & Bros., 1927).

and heartbreak because of losing him. To quote from one father: "The wife is proud of the boy. But he breaks her heart. He ain't our boy any more. He doesn't talk to us the same way. He never stays home long, and when he does he seems like a stranger. We are going to keep the youngest home. We gave two to the church already."

The very process of making a priest is to envelop the candidate in the ecclesiastical world, definitely to limit even the number of letters he can write to his family, to give him a new formalized language; in short, to make a new person of him, with new definitions of his wishes. This does by discipline what sects attempt to do by conversion; namely, to erase the person's past so that he may be completely mobilized for carrying out his mission.

This cutting off of the person from his home base simultaneously with his entrance into an occupation, with his change from one occupation to another, or even from one job to another, is that characteristic phenomenon of the modern division of labor which carries with it personality change. The change is ordinarily more casual than that from layman to priest, or from Pole to American. It may begin with a move from a rural to an urban community. Even if it be only the entrance into new groups in one's home community, it may lessen the contacts with the family, and the part of the family in determining one's social attitudes.

CLASSIFICATION OF UNITS IN
THE DIVISION OF LABOR

We may make a rough classification of the types of places in the division of labor according to (1) the manner in which persons enter, (2) the attitude of the person to his occupation, and (3) the implied standing of the occupation in the eyes of the community. One may be born to his place. There are still hereditary titles and prerogatives. Some are born to a life of leisure, but without the assumption that their parents were so born, or that the person may be assured by society of this position.

1. Those occupations to which a person is called or converted we may call *missions*. The more violent the call or conversion, the less are the ethics within the occupational group. One may become convinced that he is a servant with a special mission. The evangelist, for instance, proselytizes from the congregations of regular denominations; for these regular denominations have departed from the true faith. The missionary easily becomes a fanatic, inspired of God, having no earthly colleagues, and recognizing no one's salvation except his own. A remnant of this attitude may survive in old and well-established institutions. The Protestant minister vaguely hopes to convert the Catholics, and the priest rejoices over one Protestant soul brought into the fold. The missionary belongs to a cult, whether it be a healing, soul-saving, utopian social order cult, or a sacred branch of learning. Editors of organs of opinion acquire this sense of a mission. In such occupations a peculiar language and metaphysics are developed, which one may understand only when he has partaken of the emotional experience common to the group.

2. The *professions* and *near-professions*. The professions are entered by long training, ordinarily in a manner prescribed by the profession itself and sanctioned by the state. The training is assumed to be necessary to learning the science and technique essential to practice of the function of the profession. The training, however, carries with it as a by-product assimilation of the candidate to a set of professional attitudes and controls, a professional conscience and solidarity. The profession claims and aims to become a moral unit. It is a phenomenon of the modern city that an increasing number of occupations are attempting to gain for themselves the characteristics and status of professions.

3. The *enterprise* deals with a commodity. Sombart makes the point that the entrepreneur finds his function changing almost daily in the modern world. If he enters his business with the sense of a mission or of preserving some value to the world, he is in danger of being superseded by someone less hampered by traditional ideas. To carry on an enterprise it may be necessary for one to have long training of the so-called "practical" sort. If this training makes the person unfit to engage in other enterprises, he becomes something of a professional.

4. The *arts* are presumably entered by a combination of a special talent or ability plus a training in a technique.

5. The *trades* are very close to the arts; so close that some of the arts are associating themselves with the trades for mutual protection. The trade is entered presumably by the acquisition of a certain skill.

6. Beyond these types are the occupations which are called *jobs*. The method of acquiring a job of the more casual sort is simply to present one's self at the proper time and place when manpower of a certain age, sex, and perhaps a certain grade of intelligence, is wanted. The hobo himself, for all of his reputed aversion to work, has an occupation. There are certain jobs for which he is fitted and for which he is wanted.

All of these classes of occupations may demand a degree of mobility. Certain specialists within these classes are especially mobile, as casual laborers, actors, ministers, etc. Others have a technique or skill which is presumably capable of being practiced anywhere, as medicine; but medicine as actually practiced depends on local and personal acquaintance. Others are limited to places where an appreciative client exists, as the artist, the minister, etc. Another important variable in occupations is the nature of the contact of its practitioners with each other, and the nature of competition.

SOCIAL ATTITUDES AND
THE DIVISION OF LABOR

Within some occupations there may be persons who represent any one of the foregoing types of units in the division of labor. Especially is this true in the world of business. These different degrees of devotion to the business or to one's function, different degrees of casuality, status, different degrees of sensitivity to one's colleagues, represent different types. In the individual these are facts of his life-organization and of his personality.

In those who come to assume the professional attitude the occupation is represented both as a culture and a technique. The technique is developed with reference to certain objects or activities. The technique of the physician is in relation to the human body, which must be for him a different sort of object from what it is for the layman. To the layman it is a sacred thing, and an object of sentiment. To the real-estate man, real-estate law and the land itself are objects of technique. If he opposes change in real-estate law, it is not from sentiment, but as a matter of policy. In relation to its technique and the interests of those who use that technique, the occupational group tends to build up a set of collective representations, more or less peculiar to the occupation and more or less incomprehensible to the community. The interests, which the occupational group couches in a language more or less its own, are the basis of the code and policy of the occupational group. The code is the occupation's prescribed activity of the individuals within toward each other; the policy represents its relation to the community in which they operate. There is always a limit to the degree in which the code and policy of an occupation can deviate from the general culture of the community. Its members are products of a lay society. The practice of the occupation demands some degree of social sanction by the outside world.

This culture and technique, the etiquette and skill of the profession, appear in the individual as personal traits. The objects become to the individual a constellation of sacred and secular objects and attitudes. In general, we may say that the longer and more rigorous the period of initiation into an occupation, the more culture and technique are associated with it, and the more deeply impressed are its attitudes upon the person.

Some occupations are entered into and left so casually that no collective representations develop. But the casual worker himself, because of the very casual nature of his work, may develop certain characteristic traits. Although distinctly casual, waitresses seem to live together so much that they have developed a language and a set of social attitudes peculiar to themselves, individualistic though they be.[10]

PERSONALITY TYPES ON THE FRONTIER

The essential phenomenon of the frontier is a change in the division of labor. By extension of the frontier in China or India, we mean that those countries are being swept into a larger division of labor and that the hitherto local and self-sufficient division of labor is being destroyed or altered. In India, according to Messrs. Joshi and Wadia (*Money and the Money Market in India*), the nexus between the local world of India and the outside world is made by certain half-caste bankers or money-lenders, the *mahajan* and the *shroff*, who freely swindle the Indian peasant and who translate his crops into European bank credit. A Chinese student says there is a similar type of money-lender in China who literally sells his own people into the hands of the outside commercial world. In Western Canada Chinese are said to engage in the

---

10. Donovan, *op. cit.*, p. 128.

business of hiring men of their own nationality for Canadian employers of labor. These are personality types developed in the changing division of labor on a frontier. Such persons are without ethical or moral precedent. They are unscrupulous in that they operate to undermine the social and economic order of their peoples.

THE PERSON IN THE NEW OCCUPATION

In his paper on ecology last year R. D. McKenzie[11] introduced the concept, "center of dominance." Among other things the center of dominance is the place of a very great division of labor. It is, likewise, a frontier in which new occupational types develop. Among these new types is the man of finance, for the center of dominance is a center of credit and finance. Sombart gives us a picture of this new type of man who upset the existing order and brought in modern capitalism.

"The new men are as such free from the reference to the tradition of the family, of the business, of mercantile customs. Earlier large business lay mostly in the hands of aristocratic families with seigneurial tendencies, who shied anxiously before unsound changes or makeshifts, who held the view that it is more honorable to preserve than to win, who therefore were 'neophobes,' filled with a predilection for tradition. That the customs and usages which regulated the individual merchant in his behavior were very strict stands in close relationship with the essentially traditionally minded entrepreneurship. From all these bonds and barriers the upstart is free; he transforms the world freely according to his purpose. . . . The old families live in the continuity of business. . . . The new men are unscrupulous."[12]

When this new type, the financier, was just being de-

---

11. McKenzie, R. D., "The Concept of Dominance and World Organization," *American Journal of Sociology*. Vol. XXXIII (July, 1927) pp. 28-42.
12. Sombart, *op. cit.*, p. 29.

veloped, he was unscrupulous not only in his dealings with the outside world, but toward his competitors and colleagues as well. The biography of Daniel Drew,[13] an early operator on Wall Street, tells stories of boards of directors of corporations who betrayed the very companies they were supposed to represent. The life of Gary by Ida Tarbell tells something of the same story, and tells of the etiquette which in course of time this new element in economic life developed for their protection.[14] As the occupation grows older it becomes a social climber, bidding for a fixed or improved status in the community. The individuals in the occupation bear the marks of this social climbing. Once this status is gained, the individuals in it become "regulars," and the persons who attempt to break in with new techniques are in turn unscrupulous upstarts.

TYPES IN THE REAL ESTATE BUSINESS

The real estate business is a comparatively new one. In its rather brief history it has gone through part of the cycle from an upstart, unscrupulous business to a settled, somewhat respectable one. We may illustrate the types of personality in a unit of the division of labor from the real estate men of Chicago.

The realtor.—The "realtor," or regular real estate man, represents the type who has been in the business longest. He thinks, moves, and has his being in the world of real

---

13. White, Bouck. *The Book of Daniel Drew* (N.Y., 1910).
14. Tarbell, Ida. *The Life of Elbert H. Gary* (N.Y., 1925). "Judge Gary belongs to a group of powerful men who in the last fifty years have led in the creation in the United States of what we call Big Business. The most conspicuous of these leaders have been the elder Rockefeller in oil, the elder Morgan in banking, E. H. Harriman in railroads, and in the earlier half of the period, Andrew Carnegie in steel. The men of undoubted financial and commercial genius typified certain attitudes of mind toward business and were the sponsors of practices and an etiquette essential to understand if we are to have a realizing and helpful sense of the actual development and meaning and potentiality of Big Business."

estate. He is fairly well assimilated to a code of real estate ethics or practice, supports the policies which the leaders of the business conceive to be for the ultimate welfare of the trade. The real estate board is his club, and generally his only downtown club. It is among his fellows there that he has his professional or business status. He sponsors action to make it more difficult for others to get into the business and into the board. A few older members of the Chicago Real Estate Board have made almost a mission of their trade, and in so doing have well-nigh lost their business. They are occupationally conscious and jealous. Their name is intended as an advertisement of their place in the real estate world.

The real-estator.—The member of the Cook County Real Estate Board is poorer than the "realtor." He is perhaps less successful, and espouses the cause of democracy in real estate. He accuses the realtor of being a monopolist and a representative of "big interests." When he becomes more successful he usually becomes a "realtor."

The foreign-language agent.—He has a more casual connection with the real estate business. He gets his business with people of his own nationality, and lives in part by accelerating foreign invasions of native communities. The collective representations of the organized real estate world mean nothing to him. He lives in his own language group and capitalizes his acquaintance with this group. His neighbors are his clients.

The salesman.—The salesman is the casual of the real estate business. His services are enlisted by ads which assure the prospect that no experience is necessary. According to the realtor, the salesman is the lowest order of the real estate man. He came into the business because he could not get a job elsewhere. He stays only long enough to get an advance draft on commissions, and will not govern his occupational conduct in the interests of his employer or the real estate business in general. Every salesman complains of mistreatment by his former employer and of "dirty deals" given him by his fellow-salesmen. He is the Ishmael of the business; like the waitress, he accuses his fellows of having stolen his tips, and proceeds to steal theirs. He considers the formulated codes of business as checks upon his enterprise.

The promoter or boomer.—The real estate business in Chicago started in a land boom; the heads of now respectable and conservative firms were once boomers, as wild in their own day as the more recent boomers of Florida and Muscle Shoals. The boomer of today, however, is to them an upstart. He takes money from the sacred local market. The boomer, in turn, calls the conservative local real estate man a selfish, short-sighted pig. This boomer or promoter is the functionary of the land mania. In manner, he is a salesman of the most high-pressure sort; what he happens to be selling at the moment is merely incidental. His optimism turns itself with facility from one thing to another. His ethics are immediate expediency, and he is mobile, changing both the subjects and objects of his activity frequently. To him, likewise, restrictions of any sort put upon the business by law or the trade itself are a handicap.

The center of the real estate business is occupied by a group of men whose fortunes, clientele, and standing in the business are more or less secure. They are no longer upstarts. Their competitors are their bosom friends. To them, their real estate board has become almost a religious organization; it is certainly a fraternity. To be president of that board is an objective to which they look forward when they are well on in their lives and careers. One could name a group of men in the Chicago Real Estate Board who considered it a religious duty to attend meetings of the Board, to serve on its committees, etc. They clearly sought status nowhere so much as in their business group.

Especially when an occupation develops its own institution for control of the occupation, and protection of its prerogatives, is it likely to develop what we may call a culture, an etiquette, and a group within which one may attain the satisfaction of his wishes. This etiquette may be more or less incomprehensible to the outside, or lay, world. The hobo or casual, on the other hand, develops a set of attitudes and wishes such that his wishes are satisfied, not at work, but away from it. He is none the less sensitive to the opinions of people of his own occupational sort, and he undoubtedly constitutes a personality type.

3

Work and the Self

THERE ARE SOCIETIES in which custom or sanctioned rule determines what work a man of given status may do. In our society, at least one strong strain of ideology has it that a man may do any work which he is competent to do; or even that he has a right to the schooling and experience necessary to gain competence in any kind of work which he sets as the goal of his ambition. Equality of opportunity is, among us, stated very much in terms of the right to enter upon any occupation whatsoever. Although we do not practice this belief to the full, we are a people who cultivate ambition. A great deal of our ambition takes the form of getting training for kinds of work which carry more prestige than that which our fathers did. Thus a man's work is one of the things by which he is judged, and certainly one of the more significant things by which he judges himself.

Many people in our society work in named occupations. The names are a combination of price tag and calling card. One has only to hear casual conversation to sense how important these tags are. Hear a salesman, who has just been asked what he does, reply, "I am in sales work," or "I am

Rohrer, John H., and Sherif, M. (editors), *Social Psychology at the Crossroads*. New York, Harper and Bros., 1951. Pp. 313-323. Reprinted with permission.

in promotional work," not "I sell skillets." Schoolteachers sometimes turn schoolteaching into educational work, and the disciplining of youngsters and chaperoning of parties into personnel work. Teaching Sunday School becomes religious education, and the Y.M.C.A. Secretary is in "group work." Social scientists emphasize the science end of their name. These hedging statements in which people pick the most favorable of several possible names of their work imply an audience. And one of the most important things about any man is his audience, or his choice of the several available audiences to which he may address his claims to be someone of worth.

These remarks should be sufficient to call it to your attention that a man's work is one of the more important parts of his social identity, of his self; indeed, of his fate in the one life he has to live, for there is something almost as irrevocable about choice of occupation as there is about choice of a mate. And since the language about work is so loaded with value and prestige judgments, and with defensive choice of symbols, we should not be astonished that the concepts of social scientists who study work should carry a similar load, for the relation of social-science concepts to popular speech remains close in spite of our efforts to separate them. The difference is that while the value-weighting in popular speech is natural and proper, for concealment and ego-protection are of the essence of social intercourse—in scientific discourse the value-loaded concept may be a blinder. And part of the problem of method in the study of work behavior is that the people who have the most knowledge about a given occupation (let us say medicine), and from whom therefore the data for analysis must come, are the people in the occupation. They may combine in themselves a very sophisticated manipulative knowledge of the appropriate social relations, with a very strongly motivated suppression, and even repression, of the deeper truths about these relationships, and, in occupations of higher status, with great verbal skill in keeping these relationships from coming up for thought and discussion by other people. This is done in part by the use of and insistence upon loaded value words where their work is discussed.

My own experience in study of occupations illustrates the point that concepts may be blinders. My first essay into the field was a study of the real estate agents in Chicago. These highly competitive men were just at that point in their journey toward respectability at which they wished to emphasize their conversion from business-minded suspicion of one another to the professional attitude of confidence in each other coupled with a demand for confidence from the public. I started the study with the idea of finding out an answer to this familiar question, "Are these men professionals?" It was a false question, for the concept "profession" in our society is not so much a descriptive term as one of value and prestige. It happens over and over that the people who practice an occupation attempt to revise the conceptions which their various publics have of the occupation and of the people in it. In so doing, they also attempt to revise their own conception of themselves and of their work. The model which these occupations set before themselves is that of the "profession"; thus the term profession is a symbol for a desired conception of one's work and, hence, of one's self. The movement to "professionalize" an occupation is thus collective mobility of some among the people in an occupation. One aim of the movement is to rid the occupation of people who are not mobile enough to go along with the changes.

There are two kinds of occupational mobility. One is individual. The individual makes the several choices, and achieves the skills which allow him to move to a certain position in the occupational, and thus—he hopes—in the social and economic hierarchy. His choice is limited by several conditions, among which is the social knowledge available

to him at the time of crucial decision, a time which varies
for the several kinds of work.

The other kind of occupational mobility is that of a group
of people in an occupation, i.e., of the occupation itself. This
has been important in our society with its great changes of
technology, with its attendant proliferation of new occupations and of change in the techniques and social relations
of old ones. Now it sometimes happens that by the time a
person has the full social knowledge necessary to the smart-
est possible choice of occupations, he is already stuck with
one and in one. How strongly this may affect the drive for
professionalization of occupations, I don't know. I suspect
that it is a motive. At any rate, it is common in our society
for occupational groups to step their occupation up in the
hierarchy by turning it into a profession. I will not here
describe this process. Let me only indicate that in my own
studies I passed from the false question "Is this occupation
a profession?" to the more fundamental one, "What are the
circumstances in which the people in an occupation attempt to
turn it into a profession, and themselves into professional
people?" and "What are the steps by which they attempt to
bring about identification with their valued model?"

Even with this new orientation the term profession acted
as a blinder. For as I began to give courses and seminars
on occupations, I used a whole set of concepts and headings
which were prejudicial to full understanding of what work
behavior and relations are. One of them was that of the "code
of ethics," which still tended to sort people into the good
and the bad. It was not until I had occasion to undertake
study of race relations in industry that I finally, I trust, got
rid of this bias in the concepts which I used. Negro industrial workers, the chief objects of our study, performed the
kinds of work which have least prestige and which make least
pretension; yet it turned out that even in the lowest occupations people do develop collective pretensions to give their

work, and consequently themselves, value in the eyes of each other and of outsiders.

It was from these people that we learned that a common dignifying rationalization of people in all positions of a work hierarchy except the very top one is, "We in this position save the people in the next higher position above from their own mistakes." The notion that one saves a person of more acknowledged skill, and certainly of more acknowledged prestige and power, than one's self from his mistakes appears to be peculiarly satisfying. Now there grow up in work organizations rules of mutual protection among the persons in a given category and rank, and across ranks and categories. If one uses the term "code of ethics" he is likely not to see the true nature of these rules. These rules have of necessity to do with mistakes, for it is in the nature of work that people make mistakes. The question of how mistakes are handled is a much more penetrating one than any question which contains the concept "professional ethics" as ordinarily conceived. For in finding out how mistakes are handled, one must get at the fundamental psychological and social devices by which people are able to carry on through time, to live with others and with themselves, knowing that what is daily routine for them in their occupational roles may be fateful for others, knowing that one's routine mistakes, even the mistakes by which one learns better, may touch other lives at crucial points. It is in part the problem of dealing routinely with what are the crises of others. The people in lower ranks are thus using a powerful psychological weapon when they rationalize their worth and indispensability as lying in their protection of people in higher ranks from their mistakes. I suppose it is almost a truism that the people who take the larger responsibilities must be people who can face making mistakes, while punctiliousness must remain in second place. But this is a matter which has not been very seriously taken into account, as far as I know, in studies of the social drama of work.

Of course, the rules which people make to govern their behavior at work cover other problems than that of mistakes. Essentially the rules classify people, for to define situations and the proper behavior in situations one has to assign roles to the people involved. Among the most important subject matter of rules is the setting up of criteria for recognizing a true fellow-worker, for determining who it is safe and maybe even necessary to initiate into the in-group of close equals, and who must be kept at some distance. This problem is apt to be obscured by the term "colleagueship," which, although its etymology is perfect for the matter in hand, carries a certain notion of higher status, of respectability. (In pre-Hitler Germany the Social-Democratic workers called one another "Comrade." The Christian trade-unions insisted on the term "Colleague.")

Allow me to mention one other value-laden term which may act as a blinder in study of the social psychology of work, to wit, "restriction of production." This term contains a value assumption of another kind—namely, that there is someone who knows and has a right to determine the right amount of work for other people to do. If one does less, he is restricting production. Mayo[1] and others have done a good deal to analyze the phenomenon in question, but it was Max Weber[2] who—forty years ago—pointed to "putting on the brakes," as an inevitable result of the wrestling match between a man and his employer over the price he must pay with his body for his wage. In short, he suggested that no man easily yields to another full control over the amount

1. Mayo, Elton, W. *Human Problems of an Industrial Civilization.* New York, 1933.
2. Weber, Max, "Zur Psychophysik der industriellen Arbeit," in *Gesammelte Aufsätze zur Soziologie und Sozialpolitik.* Tübingen, 1924. Pp. 730-770.

of effort he must daily exert. On the other hand, there is no more characteristically human phenomenon than determined and even heroic effort to do a task which one has taken as his own. I do not mean to make the absurd implication that there could be a situation in which every man would be his own and only taskmaster. But I think we might better understand the social interaction which determines the measure of effort if we keep ourselves free of terms which suggest that it is abnormal to do less than one is asked by some reasonable authority.

You will have doubtless got the impression that I am making the usual plea for a value-free science, that is, for neutrality. Such is not my intention. Our aim is to *penetrate more deeply* into the personal and social drama of work, to understand the social and social-psychological arrangements and devices by which men make their work tolerable, or even glorious to themselves and others. I believe that much of our terminology and hence, of our problem setting, has limited our field of perception by a certain pretentiousness and a certain value-loading. Specifically we need to rid ourselves of any concepts which keep us from seeing that the essential problems of men at work are the same whether they do their work in some famous laboratory or in the messiest vat room of a pickle factory. Until we can find a point of view and concepts which will enable us to make comparisons between the junk peddler and the professor without intent to debunk the one and patronize the other, we cannot do our best work in this field.

Perhaps there is as much to be learned about the high-prestige occupations by applying to them the concepts which naturally come to mind for study of people in the most lowly kinds of work as there is to be learned by applying to other occupations the conceptions developed in connection with the highly-valued professions. Furthermore, I have come to the conclusion that it is a fruitful thing to start study of any social phenomenon at the point of least prestige. For, since prestige is so much a matter of symbols, and even of pretensions—however well merited—there goes with prestige a tendency to preserve a front which hides the inside of things; a front of names, of indirection, of secrecy (much of it necessary secrecy). On the other hand, in things of less prestige, the core may be more easy of access.

In recent years a number of my students have studied some more or less lowly occupations: apartment-house janitors, junk men, boxers, jazz musicians, osteopaths, pharmacists, etc. They have done so mainly because of their own connections with the occupations in question, and perhaps because of some problem of their own. At first, I thought of these studies as merely interesting and informative for what they would tell about people who do these humbler jobs, i.e., as American ethnology. I have now come to the belief that although the problems of people in these lines of work are as interesting and important as any other, their deeper value lies in the insights they yield about work behavior in any and all occupations. It is not that it puts one into the position to debunk the others, but simply that processes which are hidden in other occupations come more readily to view in these lowly ones. We may be here dealing with a fundamental matter of method in social science, that of finding the best possible laboratory for study of a given series of mechanisms.

Let me illustrate. The apartment-house janitor is a fellow who, in making his living, has to do a lot of other people's dirty work. This is patent. He could not hide it if he would. Now every occupation is not one but several activities; some of them are the "dirty work" of that trade. It may be dirty in one of several ways. It may be simply physically disgusting. It may be a symbol of degradation, something that wounds one's dignity.

Finally, it may be dirty work in that it in some way goes

counter to the more heroic of our moral conceptions. Dirty work of some kind is found in all occupations. It is hard to imagine an occupation in which one does not appear, in certain repeated contingencies, to be practically compelled to play a role of which he thinks he ought to be a little ashamed. Insofar as an occupation carries with it a self-conception, a notion of personal dignity, it is likely that at some point one will feel that he is having to do something that is *infra dignitate*. Janitors turned out to be bitterly frank about their physically dirty work. When asked, "What is the toughest part of your job," they answered almost to a man in the spirit of this quotation: "Garbage. Often the stuff is sloppy and smelly. You know some fellows can't look at garbage if it's sloppy. I'm getting used to it now, but it almost killed me when I started." Or as another put it, "The toughest part? It's the messing up in front of the garbage incinerator. That's the most miserable thing there is on this job. The tenants don't co-operate—them bastards. You tell them today, and tomorrow there is the same mess over again by the incinerator."

In the second quotation it becomes evident that the physical disgust of the janitor is not merely a thing between him and the garbage, but involves the tenant also. Now the tenant is the person who impinges most on the daily activity of the janitor. It is the tenant who interferes most with his own dignified ordering of his life and work. If it were not for a tenant who had broken a window, he could have got his regular Sunday cleaning done on time; if it were not for a tenant who had clogged a trap, he would not have been ignominiously called away from the head of his family table just when he was expansively offering his wife's critical relatives a second helping of porkchops, talking the while about the importance of his job. It is the tenant who causes the janitor's status pain. The physically disgusting part of the janitor's work is directly involved in his relations with other actors in his work drama.[3]

By a *contre coup,* it is by the garbage that the janitor judges, and, as it were, gets power over the tenants who high-hat him. Janitors know about hidden love-affairs by bits of torn-up letter paper; of impending financial disaster or of financial four-flushing by the presence of many unopened letters in the waste. Or they may stall off demands for immediate service by an unreasonable woman of whom they know from the garbage that she, as the janitors put it, "has the rag on." The garbage gives the janitor the makings of a kind of magical power over that pretentious villain, the tenant. I say a kind of magical power, for there appears to be no thought of betraying any individual and thus turning this knowledge into overt power. He protects the tenant, but, at least among Chicago janitors, it is not a loving protection.

Let your mind dwell on what one might hear from people in certain other occupations if they were to answer as frankly and bitterly as did the janitors. I do not say nor do I think that it would be a good thing for persons in all occupations to speak so freely on physical disgust as did these men. To do so, except in the most tightly closed circles, would create impossible situations. But we are likely to overlook the matter altogether in studying occupations where concealment is practiced, and thus get a false notion of the problems which have to be faced in such occupations, and of the possible psychological and social by-products of the solutions which are developed for the problem of disgust.

Now the delegation of dirty work to someone else is common among humans. Many cleanliness taboos, and perhaps even many moral scruples, depend for their practice upon success in delegating the tabooed activity to someone

---

3. Gold, Ray, "Janitors vs. Tenants; a status-income Dilemma," *The American Journal of Sociology,* LVII (March, 1952), pp. 487-493.

else. Delegation of dirty work is also a part of the process of occupational mobility. Yet there are kinds of work, some of them of very high prestige, in which such delegation is possible only to a limited extent. The dirty work may be an intimate part of the very activity which gives the occupation its charism, as is the case with the handling of the human body by the physician. In this case, I suppose the dirty work is somehow integrated into the whole, and into the prestige-bearing role of the person who does it. What role it plays in the drama of work relations in such a case is something to find out. The janitor, however, does not integrate his dirty work into any deeply satisfying definition of his role that might liquidate his antagonism to the people whose dirt he handles. Incidentally, we have found reason to believe that one of the deeper sources of antagonisms in hospitals is the belief of the people in the humblest jobs that the physician in charge calls upon them to do his dirty work in the name of the role of "healing the sick," although none of the prestige and little of the money reward of that role reaches them. Thus we might conceive of a classification of occupations involving dirty work into those in which it is knit into some satisfying and prestige-giving definition of role and those in which it is not. I suppose we might think of another classification into those in which the dirty work seems somehow wilfully put upon one and those in which it is quite unconnected with any person involved in the work drama.

There is a feeling among prison guards and mental-hospital attendants that society at large and their superiors hypocritically put upon them dirty work which they, society, and the superiors in prison and hospital know is necessary but which they pretend is not necessary. Here it takes the form, in the minds of people in these two lowly occupations, of leaving them to cope for twenty-four hours, day in and day out, with inmates whom the public never has to see and whom the people at the head of the organization see only episodically. There is a whole series of problems here which cannot be solved by some miracle of changing the social selection of those who enter the job (which is the usual unrealistic solution for such cases).

And this brings us to the brief consideration of what one may call the social drama of work. Most kinds of work bring people together in definable roles; thus the janitor and the tenant, the doctor and the patient, the teacher and the pupil, the worker and his foreman, the prison guard and the prisoner, the musician and his listener. In many occupations there is some category of persons with whom the people at work regularly come into crucial contact. In some occupations the most crucial relations are those with one's fellow-workers. It is they who can do most to make life sweet or sour. Often, however, it is the people in some other position. And in many there is a category of persons who are the consumers of one's work or services. It is probable that the people in the occupation will have a chronic fight for status, for personal dignity with this group of consumers of their services. Part of the social psychological problem of the occupation is the maintenance of a certain freedom and social distance from these people most crucially and intimately concerned with one's work.

In a good deal of our talk about occupations we imply that the tension between the producer and consumer of services is somehow a matter of ill-will or misunderstandings which easily might be removed. It may be that it lies a good deal deeper than that. Often there is a certain ambivalence on the side of the producer, which may be illustrated by the case of the professional jazz-musicians. The musician wants jobs and an income. He also wants his music to be appreciated, but to have his living depend upon the appreciation does not entirely please him. For he likes to think himself and other musicians the best judges of his playing. To play what pleases the audience—the paying customers, who are not, in his opinion, good judges—is a source of annoyance. It is not merely that the listeners, having poor taste, demand that he play music which he does not think is the best he can do; even when they admire him for playing in his own sweet way, he doesn't like it, for then they are getting too close—they are impinging on his private world too much. The musicians accordingly use all sorts of little devices to keep a line drawn between themselves and the audience; such as turning the musicians' chairs, in a dance hall without platform, in such a way as to make something of a barrier.[4] It is characteristic of many occupations that the people in them, although convinced that they themselves are the best judges, not merely of their own competence but also of what is best for the people for whom they perform services, are required in some measure to yield judgment of what is wanted to these amateurs who receive the services. This is a problem not only among musicians, but in teaching, medicine, dentistry, the arts, and many other fields. It is a chronic source of ego-wound and possibly of antagonism.

Related to this is the problem of routine and emergency. In many occupations, the workers or practitioners (to use both a lower and a higher status term) deal routinely with what are emergencies to the people who receive their services. This is a source of chronic tension between the two. For the person with the crisis feels that the other is trying to belittle his trouble; he does not take it seriously enough. His very competence comes from having dealt with a thousand cases of what the client likes to consider his unique trouble. The worker thinks he knows from long experience that people exaggerate their troubles. He therefore builds up devices to protect himself, to stall people off. This is the function of the janitor's wife when a tenant phones an appeal

---

4. Becker, Howard S. "The Professional Dance Musician and his Audience," *The American Journal of Sociology,* LVII (September, 1951), pp. 136-144.

or a demand for immediate attention to a leaky tap; it is also the function of the doctor's wife and even sometimes of the professor's wife. The physician plays one emergency off against the other; the reason he can't run right up to see Johnny who may have the measles is that he is, unfortunately, right at that moment treating a case of the black plague. Involved in this is something of the struggle mentioned above in various connections, the struggle to maintain some control over one's decisions of what work to do, and over the disposition of one's time and of one's routine of life. It would be interesting to know what the parish priest thinks to himself when he is called for the tenth time to give extreme unction to the sainted Mrs. O'Flaherty who hasn't committed a sin in years except that of being a nuisance to the priest, in her anxiety over dying in a state of sin. On Mrs. O'Flaherty's side there is the danger that she might die unshriven, and she has some occasion to fear that the people who shrive may not take her physical danger seriously and hence may not come quickly enough when at last her hour has come. There may indeed be in the minds of the receivers of emergency services a resentment that something so crucial to them can be a matter of a cooler and more objective attitude, even though they know perfectly well that such an attitude is necessary to competence, and though they could not stand it if the expert to whom they take their troubles were to show any signs of excitement.

4

Institutional Office
and The Person

THE CONSCIOUS FULFILLING of formally defined offices distinguishes social institutions from more elementary collective phenomena. This paper will discuss the nature of institutional offices and their relations to the peculiar roles and careers of persons.[1]

OFFICE AND ROLE

Sumner insisted that the mores differentiate, as well as standardize, behavior, for status lies in them.[2] Status assigns individuals to various accepted social categories; each category has its own rights and duties. No individual becomes a moral person until he has a sense of his own station and the ways proper to it. Status, in its active and conscious aspect, is an elementary form of office. An office is a stand-

---

The American Journal of Sociology, Vol. XLIII (November, 1937), pp. 404-413. Reprinted with permission.

1. W. G. Sumner, *The Folkways* (Boston, 1906), pars. 40, 41, 56, 61, 63, 67, *et passim;* C. H. Cooley, *Social Organization* (New York, 1909), chaps. iii, xxviii; E. Faris, "The Primary Group: Essence and Accident," *American Journal of Sociology,* XXXVIII (July, 1932), 41-50.
2. *Op. cit.,* par. 73.

ardized group of duties and privileges devolving upon a person in certain defined situations.

In current writing on the development of personality, a great deal is made of social role. What is generally meant is that the individual gets some consistent conception of himself in relation to other people. This conception, although identified with one's self as a unique being, is a social product; Cooley would have said, a product of primary group life. But role, however individual and unique, does not remain free of status. Indeed, Linton says "a role is the dynamic aspect of a status."[3] Role *is* dynamic, but it is also something more than status. Status refers only to that part of one's role which has a standard definition in the mores or in law. A status is never peculiar to the individual; it is historic. The person, in status and in institutional office, is identified with an *historic role*. The peculiar role of a prophet or a political leader may be transformed into the historic role or office of priesthood or kingship. Every office has had a history, in which the informal and unique have become formal and somewhat impersonal. The story of an institution might well be told in terms of the growth of its offices, with which have been identified the personal roles of series of individuals.

Entrance into a status is not always a matter of choice. That does not prevent persons from being aware that they are entering it, from focusing their wills upon it, or from fulfilling the attendant obligations with consciously varying degrees of skill and scruple. Status gives self-consciousness and the conscience something to bite on.[4]

---

3. Ralph Linton, *The Study of Man* (New York, 1936), chap. viii, "Status and Role."

4. B. Malinowski, in *Crime and Custom in Savage Society* (London, 1926), chap v *et passim*, attacks the notion, so prominent in evolutionary social theory, that the member of a primitive society adheres to custom unconsciously and automatically. He maintains that among the Trobriand Islanders there is considerable margin between the maximum and minimum fulfilling of obligations and that, within these limits, persons are impelled by motives very like those recognized among us. Some men

Every social order is, viewed in one way, a round of life. Anthropologists almost invariably describe it so, and show how persons of different status fit their activities into this round. But beyond routine, even in simple and stable societies, occur great ceremonial occasions and crucial enterprises. On such occasions some person or persons become the center of enhanced attention. Collective expression and effort are co-ordinated about them. Status may determine the selection of these persons, but they must perform special offices appropriate to the occasion. They become, within the limits of their offices, especially responsible for the fate of their fellows and for the integrity of their communities.[5]

The person who fills such a great office is judged not as the common run of mankind but with reference to his predecessors in office and to the popular conception of what the office should be. He is exposed to special demands. He is also protected, insofar as the office sets the limits of his responsibility, from both the bludgeons of critics and the sharp thrusts of his own conscience.

Objective differentiation of duty reaches its ultimate rigidity in ritual office. The subjective aspect of such rigidity is punctiliousness.[6] The responsibilities of ritual office are so clear-cut as to allow the incumbent a feeling of assurance that he is doing his whole duty. The anxiety lest he fall short is but the greater.[7] Anxiety and responsibility are alike focused

---

show an excess of zeal and generosity, banking upon a return in goods and prestige. He points also to a conflict of offices embodied in one person; a man is at once affectionate parent of his own children and guardian of the property and interests of his sister's children. Malinowski suggests that the man is often aware of this conflict.

5. See R. Redfield, *Chan Kom, a Maya Village* (Washington, 1934), pp. 153-59, for description of the *fiesta* and the office of *cargador;* B. Malinowski, *Argonauts of the Western Pacific* (London, 1922), for the office of the chieftain in canoe-building and expeditions, and that of the magician in gardening.

6. Sumner, *op. cit.*, par. 67.

7. The psychoanalysts trace ritual to anxieties arising from unconscious guilt. In compulsion neurosis the individual ceaselessly performs rituals of penitence and of washing away one's sins (see A. Fenichel, *Hysterien*

upon the office, as something transcending the individual. The incumbent tends to be impatient of the criticisms of others. He wards them off by declaring that whoever criticizes him attacks the sacred office.

In the performance of ritual one may realize profoundly that he, even he, is playing a historic role; he may be transfigured in an ecstasy in which his personal attributes are merged with those of the office. Each meticulous gesture bursts with symbolic meaning. E. Boyd Barrett writes thus of his feeling while celebrating his first mass.

> On the snow-white altar cloth before me lay a chalice of wine and on a paten a wafer of unleavened bread. Presently *at my words,* at my repetition of the eternal formula of consecration, the wine would become the blood of Christ, and the bread the body of Christ. My hands, soiled and sinful though they were, would be privileged to raise aloft in adoration the Son of God, the Saviour of the world. . . . Surely the words "Sanctus! Sanctus! Sanctus!" were none too sacred to pronounce in presence of this mystery of mysteries. . . . My first mass was an ecstasy of joy. . . . I gave myself confidently and wholeheartedly to God and I felt that He gave himself to me.[8]

While devotion and sense of office may be at their maximum in such moments, judgment is in abeyance. It is in the nature of ritual that it should be, since each action is part of a sacred whole. Furthermore, rituals are performed under compulsion often backed by a vow. A vow allows no turning back, no changing of the mind, no further exercise of judgment.[9]

---

und Zwangsneurosen, Vienna, 1931, chap. iv). J. Piaget, in *The Moral Judgment of the Child* (London, 1932), finds that young children play marbles as ritual before they play it as a game. In this early stage they observe punctiliously such rules as they know, attributing their origin to their fathers, the city alderman, and God. They are quick to accuse and facile at self-excuse, but show little regard for their fellow-players.

8. *Ex-Jesuit* (London, 1930), p. 124. Published in the U. S. A. as *The Magnificent Illusion.*

9. See W. G. Sumner, *War and Other Essays,* "Mores of the Present

An office may eventually become so ritualistic that the successive incumbents are but symbols rather than responsible agents. A rigid etiquette is observed in approaching them, and sentiments of reverence become so intense that the office is worshiped. This final point of impersonal institution of an office is reached at the cost of the more active functions of leadership. In ongoing collective life, contingencies arise to require decisions. Even a ritual may not go on without a stage-manager. Furthermore, every ritual is proper to an occasion. The occasion must be recognized and met. An office may become purely symbolic only if the meeting of contingencies is allocated to some other office.[10]

---

and Future," p. 157 (New Haven, 1911) in which he says: "One of the most noteworthy and far-reaching features in modern mores is the unwillingness to recognize a vow or to enforce a vow by any civil or ecclesiastical process. . . . In modern mores it is allowed that a man may change his mind as long as he lives." The belief that a man may change his mind is an essentially secular attitude. Catholic doctrine recognizes this, by distinguishing resolutions, promises, and vows. Vows are the most sacred, since they are promises to God. "A subsequent change in one's purpose is a want of respect to God; it is like taking away something that has been dedicated to Him, and committing sacrilege in the widest sense of the word." Resolutions are mere present intentions, without a commitment; promises between man and man or to the saints should be kept, but the breach is not so serious as that of a vow (*The Catholic Encyclopedia*, Vol. XV, "Vows"). It is perhaps the residue of the compulsion of a vow that gives ex-priests the sense of being marked men. See E. Boyd Barrett, *op. cit.* Ordinary life may be something of an anticlimax for these men once dedicated to holy office. Such men are also suspect. A French-Canadian recently dismissed all that a certain psychologist might say by remarking, "He is a man who once wore the cloth."

There are many instances in sociological literature of the profound changes in an institution that accompany the decline of compulsion in its offices. Redfield, *op. cit.*, tells how in towns and cities the *fiesta* becomes something of a secular enterprise. No longer is it a sacred festival, led by a *cargador* who accepted "the holy burden" from his predecessor. The Webbs, in *English Local Government: the Parish and the County* (London, 1906), describe a similar decline of the sense of obligation to serve as parish officers in growing industrial towns.

10. Max Weber, in his "Politik als Beruf" (*Gesammelte politische Schriften*, Munich, 1921, pp. 396-450), essays a natural history of various types of political office. He shows how certain offices, as that of sultan, became purely symbolic, while the wielding of political power and the risk of making mistakes were assumed by others. The position of the emperor of Japan is similar; the emperor is divine, but he speaks only through the

Coming down to earth, the person cannot, apart from ritual, escape judgments. His peculiar social role asserts itself and may come into conflict with the office which he fills. The fusion of personal role and office is perhaps never complete save in ritual.

One of the extreme forms in which one's personal role appears is that of a call or peculiar mission. The person's conception of his mission may carry him beyond the conception which others have of his office. As an office becomes defined, there arise devices by which one's fellows decide whether one is the person fit to fill it. The first leader of a sect may be "called" to his task; his successors, too, are "called," but the validity of the call is decided by other men, as well as by himself.[11] Thus the "call," a subjective assurance and compulsion, is brought under the control of one's fellows. But the sense of mission may be so strong that it makes the person impatient of the discipline exercised by his colleagues.[12]

There are other ways in which personal role and office may conflict. It is sufficient for our present purposes to sug-

---

voices of men. It is not suggested that these two features do not sometimes appear in the same office. They do, as in the papacy. Offices vary in their proportions of symbol and action.

11. See the *Catholic Encyclopedia*, Vol. XV, "Vocation." While the Catholic church admits the possibility that divine light may be shed so abundantly upon a soul as to render deliberation about the validity of a vocation unnecessary in some cases, it does not regard such inner assurance necessary to vocation. The spiritual director is to discover and develop the germ of vocation by forming the character and encouraging "generosity of the will." The church insists that two wills should concur before one can enter the clergy: the will of the individual and the will of the church. The latter is "external vocation," which is "the admission of the candidate in due form by competent authority."

12. The ardor of a person with a peculiar mission may become an insufferable reproach to his colleagues and contain a trace of insubordination to his superiors. The neophyte who is too *exalté* can be borne, but a certain relaxation of ardor is demanded in course of time. In a well-established institution, ardor must be kept within the limits demanded by authority and decorum; it may not necessarily reach the state in which "men, fearing to outdo their duty, leave it half done," as Goldsmith said of the English clergy in his essay on education.

gest that the very sense of personal role which leads one into an institutional office may make him chafe under its bonds. The economy of energy and will, devotion and judgment, peculiar to the individual does not completely disappear when he is clothed with an established, even a holy, office. The more secular offices make fewer formal demands upon the individual; they require less suppression of the individuality. They are less symbolic and more subject to the test of effectiveness in action. A free, secular society, from this point of view, is one in which the individual may direct his energies toward new objects; one in which he may even succeed in creating a new office, as well as in changing the nature and functions of existing ones.

CAREER AND OFFICE

In any society there is an appropriate behavior of the child at each age. Normal development of personality involves passing in due time from one status to another. Some stages in this development are of long duration; others are brief. While some are thought of as essentially preparatory, and their length justified by some notion that the preparation for the next stage requires a set time, they are, nevertheless, conventional.

In a relatively stable state of society, the passage from one status to another is smooth and the experience of each generation is very like that of its predecessor. In such a state the expected rate of passage from one status to another and an accompanying scheme of training and selection of those who are to succeed to instituted offices determine the ambitions, efforts, and accomplishments of the individual. In a society where major changes are taking place, the sequence of generations in an office and that of offices in the life of the person are disturbed. A generation may be lost by disorder lasting only for the few years of passage through one phase.

However one's ambitions and accomplishments turn, they involve some sequence of relations to organized life. In a highly and rigidly structured society, a career consists, objectively, of a series of status and clearly defined offices. In a freer one, the individual has more latitude for creating his own position or choosing from a number of existing ones; he has also less certainty of achieving any given position. There are more adventurers and more failures; but unless complete disorder reigns, there will be typical sequences of position, achievement, responsibility, and even of adventure. The social order will set limits upon the individual's orientation of his life, both as to direction of effort and as to interpretation of its meaning.

Subjectively, a career is the moving perspective in which the person sees his life as a whole and interprets the meaning of his various attributes, actions, and the things which happen to him. This perspective is not absolutely fixed either as to points of view, direction, or destination. In a rigid society the child may, indeed, get a fixed notion of his destined station. Even in our society he may adopt a line of achievement as his own to the point of becoming impervious to conflicting ambitions. Consistent lines of interest and tough conceptions of one's destined role may appear early in life.[13]

13. Psychoanalysts trace to very lowly motives the lines of consistency in the individual's conception of his life and the way in which he disciplines and marshals his efforts. Their more important point is that these phenomena rise out of intimate family relationships. They also use the term "mobility of the libido" (cf. Klein, "The Role of the School in the Libidinal Development of the Child." *International Journal of Psychoanalysis,* V [1924], 312-31) to indicate the child's capacity to transfer his affections and energies to objects in a larger world as he grows and extends his circle of activity. A great deal, however, remains to be done in the way of understanding the bearing of early experiences on the subsequent careers of persons. It is evident that the age, as well as the frequency, of appearance of a sense of career varies greatly from family to family and from class to class. The pressure on children to discipline themselves for careers likewise varies; the psychological by-products of these pressures want studying, for they seem sometimes to thwart the ends they seek.

Whatever the importance of early signs of budding careers, they rarely remain unchanged by experience. The child's conception of the social order in which adults live and move is perhaps more naïve than are his conceptions of his own abilities and peculiar destiny. Both are revised in keeping with experience. In the interplay of his maturing personality and an enlarging world the individual must keep his orientation.

Careers in our society are thought of very much in terms of jobs, for these are the characteristic and crucial connections of the individual with the institutional structure. Jobs are not only the accepted evidence that one can "put himself over"; they also furnish the means whereby other things that are significant in life may be procured. But the career is by no means exhausted in a series of business and professional achievements. There are other points at which one's life touches the social order, other lines of social accomplishment —influence, responsibility, and recognition.

A woman may have a career in holding together a family or in raising it to a new position. Some people of quite modest occupational achievements have careers in patriotic, religious, and civic organizations. They may, indeed, budget their efforts toward some cherished office of this kind rather than toward advancement in their occupations. It is possible to have a career in an avocation as well as in a vocation.

Places of influence in our greater noncommercial organizations are, however, open mainly to those who have acquired prestige in some other field. The governors of universities are selected partly on the basis of their business successes. A recent analysis of the governing boards of settlement houses in New York City shows that they are made up of people with prestige in business and professional life,

---

See H. D. Lasswell, *World Politics and Personal Insecurity* (New York, 1935), pp. 210-12, for a discussion of "career lines."

as well as some leisure and the ability to contribute something to the budget.[14]

It would be interesting to know just how significant these offices appear to the people who fill them; and further, to whom they regard themselves responsible for the discharge of their functions. Apart from that question, it is of importance that these offices are by-products of achievements of another kind. They are prerogatives and responsibilities acquired incidentally; it might even be said that they are exercised ex officio or *ex statu.*

The interlocking of the directorates of educational, charitable, and other philanthropic agencies is due perhaps not so much to a cabal as to the very fact that they are philanthropic. Philanthropy, as we know it, implies economic success; it comes late in a career. It may come only in the second generation of success. But when it does come, it is quite as much a matter of assuming certain prerogatives and responsibilities in the control of philanthropic institutions as of giving money. These prerogatives and responsibilities form part of the successful man's conception of himself and part of the world's expectation of him.[15]

Another line of career characteristic of our society and its institutional organization is that which leads to the position of "executive." It is a feature of our society that a great many of its functions are carried out by corporate bodies. These bodies must seek the approval and support of the public, either through advertising or propaganda. Few institutions enjoy such prestige and endowments that they can forego continued reinterpretation of their meaning and value to the community. This brings with it the necessity of having some set of functionaries who will act as promoters and

---

14. Kennedy A. J., Farra, K., and Associates, *Social Settlements in New York* (New York, 1935), chap. xiv; T. Veblen, *The Higher Learning in America* (New York, 1918), p. 72 *et passim.*

15. The Junior League frankly undertakes to train young women of leisure for their expected offices in philanthropic agencies.

propagandists as well as administrators. Even such a traditional profession as medicine and such an established organization as the Roman Catholic church must have people
of this sort. By whatever names they be called, their function
is there and may be identified.

Sometimes, as in the case of executive secretaries of medical associations, these people are drawn from the ranks of
the profession. In other cases they are drawn from outside.
University presidents have often been drawn from the clergy.
In the Y.M.C.A. the chief executive officer is quite often not
drawn from the ranks of the "secretaries." But whether or
not that be the case, the functions of these executive officers
are such that they do not remain full colleagues of their professional associates. They are rather liaison officers between
the technical staff, governing boards, and the contributing
and clientele publics. Their technique is essentially a political
one; it is much the same whether they act for a trade association, the Y.M.C.A., a hospital, a social agency, or a university. There is, indeed, a good deal of competition among
institutions for men who have this technique, and some movement of them from one institution to another. They are also
men of enthusiasm and imagination. The institution becomes
to them something in which dreams may be realized.[16]

These enthusiastic men, skilled in a kind of politics necessary in a philanthropic, democratic society, often come to
blows with the older hierarchical organization of the institutions with which they are connected. Therein lies their
importance to the present theme. They change the balance
of power between the various functioning parts of institu-

---

16. The reports made by the American Association of University Professors on conflicts between professors and college presidents sometimes
reveal in an interesting way the characteristics of both and of the offices
they fill. See *Bulletin of the American Association of University Professors*, XXI (March, 1935), pp. 224-66, "The University of Pittsburgh";
XIX (November, 1933), pp. 416-38, "Rollins College."

tions. They change not only their own offices but those of others.

Studies of certain other types of careers would likewise throw light on the nature of our institutions—as, for instance, the road to political office by way of fraternal orders, labor unions, and patriotic societies. Such careers are enterprises and require a kind of mobility, perhaps even a certain opportunism, if the person is to achieve his ambitions. These ambitions themselves seem fluid, rather than fixed upon solid and neatly defined objectives. They are the opposites of bureaucratic careers, in which the steps to be taken for advancement are clearly and rigidly defined, as are the prerogatives of each office and its place in the official hierarchy.[17] It may be that there is a tendency for our social structure to become rigid, and thus for the roads to various positions to be more clearly defined. Such a trend would make more fateful each turning-point in a personal career. It might also require individuals to cut their conceptions of themselves to neater, more conventional, and perhaps smaller patterns.

However that may be, a study of careers—of the moving perspective in which persons orient themselves with reference to the social order, and of the typical sequences and concatenations of office—may be expected to reveal the nature and "working constitution" of a society. Institutions are but the forms in which the collective behavior and collective action of people go on. In the course of a career the person finds his place within these forms, carries on his active life with reference to other people, and interprets the meaning of the one life he has to live.

17. Mannheim would limit the term "career" to this type of thing. Career success, he says, can be conceived only as *Amtskarriere*. At each step in it one receives a neat package of prestige and power whose size is known in advance. Its keynote is security; the unforeseen is reduced to the vanishing-point ("Über das Wesen und die Bedeutung des wirtschaftlichen Erfolgsstrebens," *Archiv für Sozialwissenschaft und Sozialpolitik*, LXIII [1930], p. 458 ff.).

5

Social Role
and The Division of Labor

ALL OF THE MANY WAYS in which the work of human beings is studied lead back at some point to the obvious, yet
infinitely subtle, fact of the division of labor. What is a
job description if not a statement of what one worker, rather
than another, does or is supposed to do? Similar reference to
division of labor lies implicitly in study of the number and
migrations of the labor force, of motive and effort, of basic
capacities and the learning of skills, and in analysis of the
price of labor, services and goods.

The division of labor, in its turn, implies interaction; for
it consists not in the sheer difference of one man's kind of
work from that of another, but in the fact that the different
tasks and accomplishments are parts of a whole to whose
product all, in some degree, contribute. And wholes, in the
human social realm as in the rest of the biological and in the
physical realm, have their essence in interaction. Work as
social interaction is the central theme of sociological and social psychological study of work.

Social role, the other term in my title, is useful only to

Bulletin of the Committee on Human Development, University of
Chicago, 1955. Pp. 32-38. Reprinted by permission.

the extent that it facilitates analysis of the parts played by individuals in the interaction which makes up some sort of social whole. I am not sure that I would put up much of an argument against the objection that it is not a very useful term, provided the objector has a better one to refer to the same complex of phenomena. I would argue vociferously, however, if the objector implied either that social interaction is not an ever-present and crucial feature of human work, or that the social-psychological description of a division of labor implied by the term social role is of less importance than a description in terms of techniques. I would mention to the objector that even those who work in solitude are often interacting with a built-in father or with God himself, who is known to be worse than any flesh-and-blood slavedriver; and that those who toil upward in the night while their companions sleep may quite simply be seeking access to an as yet unknown, but more admired set of companions or colleagues.

I will not define or further belabor these terms, social role and the division of labor, but rather illustrate some of their dimensions from those kinds of work which consist in doing something for, or to, people. I say *for* or *to* people intentionally, but not cynically. Any child in any school will sometimes believe that something is being done to him rather than for him; the boy in a reform school nearly always thinks so. The patient in a mental hospital is often convinced that things are being done *to* him *for* someone else; although it may be in the nature of his illness so to believe, he may nevertheless often be right. Even the person suffering from tuberculosis, although he knows he is ill and willingly undergoes treatment, considers that many of the rules of society and of the hospital, and even some parts of the treatment are done *to* him, rather than *for* his benefit. Even in short-term illnesses, the patient may view as indignities some of the things allegedly done for his recovery. At the least, he may think that they are done for the convenience of those who work in the hospital rather than for his comfort. These are but some of the simpler ambiguities in those kinds of work called personal or professional services. Perhaps it is well to recall that the opposite of service is disservice, and that the line between them is thin, obscure and shifting.

In many of the things which people do for one another, the *for* can be changed to *to* by a slight over-doing or by a shift of mood. The discipline necessary to that degree of order and quiet which will allow study in a class-room can easily turn into something perceived by the children as perverse and cruel; their perceptions may be truer than the teacher's own self-perception. Wherever a modicum of power to discipline by tongue or force is essential to one's assigned task, the temptation to over-use it and even to get pleasure from it may be present, no matter whether one be a teacher, an attendant in a mental hospital, or a prison guard. The danger of major distortion of relationship and function within the framework of a formal office lurks wherever people go or are sent for help or correction: the school-room, the clinic, the operating room, the confessional booth, the undertaking parlor all share this characteristic. Whatever terms we eventually may use to describe social interaction at work must be such that they will allow these subtle distortions of role or function to be brought to light and related to whatever are their significant correlates in personalities or situations.

Another feature of the kinds of work in question lies in the peculiar ambiguities with respect to what is seen as honorable, respectable, clean and prestige-giving as against what is less honorable or respectable, and what is mean or dirty. The term profession in its earlier and more restricted usage referred to a very few occupations of high learning and prestige, whose practitioners did things for others. Law and medicine are the prototypes. Yet both of them have always required some sort of alliance, or, at least, some sort of terms with the lowliest and most despised of human occupations. It is not merely in Dickens' novels that lawyers have truck with process-servers, informants, spies and thugs. What the learned lawyers argue before an Appellate Court (and I hear that the cases used in law schools are almost all from Appellate Courts) is but a purified distillate of some human mess. A lawyer may be asked whether he and his client come into court with clean hands; when he answers, "yes," it may mean that someone else's hands are of necessity a bit grubby. For not only are some quarrels more respectable, more clean, than others; but also some of the kinds of work involved in the whole system (gathering evidence, getting clients, bringing people to court, enforcing judgments, making the compromises that keep cases out of court) are more respected and more removed from temptation and suspicion than others. In fact, the division of labor among lawyers is as much one of respectability (hence of self concept and role) as of specialized knowledge and skills. One might even call it a moral division of labor, if one keeps in mind that the term means not simply that some lawyers, or people in the various branches of law work, are more moral than others; but that the very demand for highly scrupulous and respectable lawyers depends in various ways upon the availability of less scrupulous people to attend to the less respectable legal problems of even the best people. I do not mean that the good lawyers all consciously delegate their dirty work to others (although many do). It is rather a game of live and let live; a game, mind you, hence interaction, even though it be a game of keeping greater than chance distances.

As the system of which the lawyer's work is part reaches down into the nether regions of the unrespectable and outward to the limbo of guile and force, which people may think necessary but do not admire, so the physician's work touches the world of the morally and ritually, but more especially of the physically unclean. Where his work leaves off, that of the undertaker begins; in some cultures and epochs they have shared the monopoly of certain functions and certain occult arts. The physician has always had also to have some connection (even though it be again the connection of competition or of studied avoidance) with the abortionist, with the "quacks" who deal with obscure and "social" diseases, as well as with the lesser occupations which also treat physical and mental troubles: the midwife, who has in certain places and times been suspected of being willing to do her work a bit prematurely; the blood-letter, who has at times been also the lowly barber; the bonesetter, who in mediaeval Italy was also the smith; and the masseur and keeper of baths, who is often suspected of enjoying his work too much. If the physician has high prestige—and he has had it at various times in history, although perhaps never more so than now—it is not so much *sui generis,* as by virtue of his place in the particular pattern of the medical division of labor at the time. Two features of that division of labor at present are (1) that the level of public confidence in the technical competence and good faith of the medical system is very high and (2) that nearly all of the medical functions have been drawn into a great system of interlocking institutions over which physicians have an enormous measure of control. (Only abortion remains outside, and even that can be said only with some qualification.)

It is also a division of labor notorious for its rigid hierarchy. The ranking has something to do with the relative cleanliness of functions performed. The nurses, as they successfully rise to professional standing, are delegating the more lowly of their traditional tasks to aides and maids. No one is so lowly in the hospital as those who handle soiled linen; none so low in the mental hospital as the attendant, whose work combines some tasks that are not clean with potential use of force. But if there is no system in which the theme of uncleanliness is so strong, likewise there is none in which it is so strongly compensated for. Physical cleanliness of the human organism depends upon balances easily upset; the physician and his co-workers operate at the margins where these balances are, in fact, often upset. To bring back health (which is cleanliness) is the great miracle. Those who work the miracle are more than absolved from the potential uncleanliness of their tasks; but those who perform the lowly tasks without being recognized as among the miracle-workers fare badly in the prestige rating. And this gives us a good case for rubbing in the point that the division of labor is more than a technical phenomenon; that there are infinite social-psychological nuances in it.

Actually, in the medical world there are two contrary trends operating simultaneously. As medical technology develops and changes, particular tasks are constantly downgraded; that is, they are delegated by the physician to the nurse. The nurse in turn passes them on to the maid. But occupations and people are being upgraded, within certain limits. The nurse moves up nearer the doctor in techniques and devotes more of her time to supervision of other workers. The practical nurse is getting more training, and is beginning to insist on the prerogatives which she believes should go with the tasks she performs. New workers come in at the bottom of the hierarchy to take over the tasks abandoned by those occupations which are ascending the mobility ladder. Others come in outside the hierarchy as new kinds of technology (photography, electronics, physics) find a place in the medical effort. Satisfactory definitions of role for these new people are notoriously lacking, and that in a system in which rigidly defined roles and ranks are the rule. Here we have indeed a good case for illustrating the point that a role definition of a division of labor is necessary to complement any technical description of it. And the question arises of the effect of changes in technical division upon the roles involved. Sometimes a desired change of role is validated by a change in technical tasks (the nurses are an excellent example).

Sometimes a change in technical division creates a role problem, or a series of them. I think we may go further and say that when changes of either kind get under way the repercussions will be felt beyond the positions immediately affected, and may indeed touch every position in the system. Some roles in a division of labor may be more sensitive to changes in technique than are others. It seems probable, for instance, that some aspects of the basic relationships of nurse, physician and patient will not be greatly altered by the shifting of technical tasks from one to the other and from both of them to other people in the medical system. (I purposely included the patient, for he has a part in the medical division of labor, too.)

There will probably always be in this system, as in others, someone whose role it is to make ultimate decisions, with all the risks that go with them and with all the protections necessary. This is the role of the physician. He has and jealously guards more authority than he can, in many cases, actually assume. There will probably always be in the system, complementary to this position, another of the right-hand-man order; a position which defers to the first but which, informally, often must exceed its authority in order to protect the interests of all concerned. The nurse occupies this position. When the doctor isn't there, she may do some necessary thing which requires his approval—and get the approval when he comes back. She is the right-hand man of the physician, even and perhaps especially when he isn't there. The nurse also sometimes fires furnaces and mends the plumbing, i.e., she does tasks of people below her or outside the role hierarchy of medicine. It hurts her, but she does it. Her place in the division of labor is essentially that of doing in a responsible way whatever necessary things are in danger of not being done at all. The nurse would not like this definition, but she ordinarily in practice rises to it. I believe that, if we were to take a number of systems of work in which things are done for people we could dig out a series of roles or positions which

could be described in some such way, and could see the consequences for the roles of changes in technique and in other
roles in the system. And I would defend the term role as a
fair starting term in such an enterprise; for it suggests a part
in a whole act involving other people playing, well or badly,
their expected parts.

I have been saying, in various rather indirect ways, that
no line of work can be fully understood outside the social
matrix in which it occurs or the social system of which it is
part. The system includes, in most and perhaps in all cases,
not merely the recognized institutional complex but reaches
out and down into other parts of society. As in the case of
law and even in medicine, there are usually some connections
which we cannot easily or do not willingly follow out. There
are also ambiguities and apparent contradictions in the combinations of duties of any one occupation or position in an
occupational system.

One of the commoner failures in study of work is to
overlook part of the interactional system. We speak of the
physician and patient as a social system (as did the late Dr.
L. J. Henderson in an article by that name),[1] or at most include the nurse; or we speak of teacher and pupil, lawyer
and client, and the like. Certainly in some occupations there
is some basic relation such as these; a relation which is partly
reality, partly stereotype, partly ideal nostalgically attributed
to a better past or sought after in a better future. Perhaps the
commonest complaint of people in the professions which perform a service for others, is that they are somehow prevented
from doing their work as it should be done. Someone interferes
with this basic relation. The teacher could teach better were
it not for parents who fail in their duty or school boards who
interfere. Psychiatrists would do better if it were not for families, stupid public officials, and ill-trained attendants. Nurses

---

1. Henderson, L. J., "Physician and Patient as a Social System," *The
New England Journal of Medicine*, 212 (November 1937), pp. 404-13.

would do more nursing if it were not for administrative duties, and the carelessness of aides and maintenance people. Part of the complained-of interference is merely institutional. The institutional matrix in which things are done for people is certainly becoming more complex in most professional fields; there are more and more kinds of workers in a division of labor ever changing in its boundaries between one person's work and another's. But it is not so much the numbers of people who intervene that seems to bother the professional most; it is rather the differing conceptions of what the work really is or should be, of what mandate has been given by the public, of what it is possible to accomplish and by what means; as well as of the particular part to be played by those in each position, their proper responsibilities and rewards. Compared to the restrictions, resistances and distortions of purpose, assignments, and efforts in a school, a mental hospital, a social agency or a prison, the much studied restriction of production in a factory is simplicity itself. In the factory, there is at least fair consensus about what the object produced shall be. There is often no such consensus in institutions where things are done for or to people.

Every one, or nearly every one of the many important services given people by professionals in our times is given in a complex institutional setting. The professional must work with a host of non-professionals (and the professionals ordinarily are shortsighted enough to use that pejorative term ad nauseam). These other workers bring into the institutional complex their own conceptions of what the problem is, their own conceptions of their rights and privileges, and of their careers and life-fate. The philosophy—of illness, crime, reform, mental health, or whatever—which they bring in is often that of another class or element of the population than that to which the professional belongs or aspires. Like most humans, they do not completely accept the role-definitions handed down from above, but in communication among their own kind and in interaction with the people served, treated, or handled, work out their own definition. They build up an ethos, and a system of rationalizations for the behavior they consider proper given the hazards and contingencies of their own positions. The proper study of the division of labor will include a look at any system of work from the points of view of all the kinds of people involved in it, whether their position be high or low, whether they are at the center or near the periphery of the system. And those who seek to raise standards of practice (and their own status) in the occupations and institutions which do things for people would do well to study, in every case, what changes in the other positions or roles in the system will be wrought by changes in their own, and what problems will be created for other people by every new solution of one of their own problems.

6

Licence and Mandate

AN OCCUPATION consists, in part, of a successful claim of some people to *licence* to carry out certain activities which others may not, and to do so in exchange for money, goods or services. Those who have such licence will, if they have any sense of self-consciousness and solidarity, also claim a *mandate* to define what is proper conduct of others toward the matters concerned with their work. The licence may be nothing more than permission to carry on certain narrowly technical activities, such as installing electrical equipment, which it is thought dangerous to allow laymen to do. It may, however, include the right to live one's life in a style somewhat different from that of most people. The mandate may go no further than successful insistence that other people stand back and give the workers a bit of elbow room while they do their work. It may, as in the case of the modern physician, include a successful claim to supervise and determine the conditions of work of many kinds of people; in this case, nurses, technicians and the many others involved in maintaining the modern medical establishment. In the extreme case it may, as in the priesthood in strongly Catholic countries, include the right to control the thoughts and beliefs of whole populations with respect to nearly all the major concerns of life.

Licence, as an attribute of an occupation, is ordinarily thought of as legal permission to carry on a kind of work. There is a great body of jurisprudence having to do with the matter of licence, both in principle and as it occurs in various occupations. I have in mind something both broader and deeper, something that is sometimes implicit and of undefined boundaries. For it is very difficult to define the boundaries of the licence to carry on a certain kind of activity. What I am talking of is a basic attribute of society. Occupations here offer us an extreme and highly lighted instance of a general aspect of all human societies. For society, by its very nature, consists of both allowing and expecting some people to do things which other people are not allowed or expected to do. All occupations—most of all those considered professions and perhaps those of the underworld—include as part of their very being a licence to deviate in some measure from common modes of behavior. Professions also, perhaps more than other kinds of occupations, claim a legal, moral and intellectual mandate. Not merely do the practitioners, by virtue of gaining admission to the charmed circle of colleagues, individually exercise the licence to do things others do not do, but collectively they presume to tell society what is good and right for the individual and for society at large in some aspect of life. Indeed, they set the very terms in which people may think about this aspect of life. The medical profession, for instance, is not content merely to define the terms of medical practice. It also tries to define for all of us the very nature of health and disease. When the presumption of a group to a broad mandate of this kind is explicitly or implicitly granted as legitimate, a profession has come into being.

The understanding of the nature and extent of both licence and mandate, of their relations to each other and of the circumstances in which they expand or contract is a crucial area of study not merely of occupations, but of society itself. In such licences and mandates we have the prime manifestation of the *moral division of labor;* that is, of the processes by which differing moral functions are distributed among the members of society, both as individuals and as kinds or categories of individuals. Moral functions differ from each other both in kind and in measure. Some people seek and get special responsibility for defining the values and for establishing and enforcing social sanctions over some aspect of life. The differentiation of moral and social functions involves both the setting of the boundaries of realms of social behavior and the allocation of responsibility and power over them. One may indeed speak of jurisdictional disputes concerning the rights and the responsibilities of various occupations and categories of people in defining and maintaining the rules of conduct concerning various aspects of personal and social life.

In these pages I mean to illustrate some of the problems of licence and mandate, and some of the relations between them.

Many occupations cannot be carried out without guilty knowledge. The priest cannot mete out penance without becoming an expert in sin; else how may he know the mortal from the venial. To carry out his mandate to tell people what books they may or may not read, and what thoughts and beliefs they must espouse or avoid, he must become a connoisseur of the forbidden, as well of the right and holy. Only a master theologian can think up dangerously subtle heresies; hence is Satan of necessity a fallen angel. Few laymen have the sophistication to think up either original or very seductive heresies. The poor priest—at least in the Roman Catholic Church—as part of the very exchange involved in his licence to hear confessions and to absolve people of their sins, and in his mandate to tell us what is what with respect to matters moral and spiritual, has constantly to convince the layman that he does not yield to the temptations of his privileged position; he puts on a uniform which makes him a marked man and lives a celibate existence. These are compensating or counter-deviations from the common ways of dressing and living. They probably would not be admired, and perhaps would not even be tolerated, if practiced by people who have no special social functions to justify such peculiar conduct. The priest, in short, has both intellectual and moral leeway, and perhaps must have them if he is to carry out the rest of his licence and if he is to merit his great mandate. He carries a burden of guilty knowledge.

The lawyer, the policeman, the physician, the newspaper reporter, the scientist, the scholar, the diplomat, the private secretary, all of them must have licence to get—and in some degree, to keep secret—some order of guilty, or at least potentially embarrassing and dangerous knowledge. It may be guilty in that it is knowledge that the layman would be obliged to reveal, or in that the withholding of it from the public or from legal authorities compromises, or may compromise, the integrity of the man who has it and who does withhold it. Such is the case of the policeman who keeps connections with the underworld and who fails to report some misdemeanors or crimes of which he knows. He may, of course, defend himself by saying that if he lets the small fish go he may be better able to catch the big one. Such also is the case of the diplomat who has useful friends abroad. Most occupations rest upon some explicit or implicit bargain between the practitioner and the individuals with whom he works, and between the occupation as a whole and society at large about receiving, keeping and the giving out of information gathered in course of one's work. The licence to keep this bargain is of the essence of many occupations. It is also a fundamental feature of all social and moral division of labor, thus of the social and moral order itself.

The prototype of all guilty knowledge, however, is a way of looking at things different from that of most people and consequently potentially shocking to the lay mind. Every occupation must look in a relative way at some order of events, objects, and ideas. These must be classified. To be classified they must be seen comparatively. Their behavior must be analyzed and, if possible, predicted. A suitable technical language must be developed so that colleagues may talk among themselves about these things. This technical—therefore relative—attitude will have to be adopted toward the very people one serves; no profession can do its work without licence to talk in shocking terms about its clients and their problems. Sometimes an occupation must adopt this objective, comparative attitude toward things which are very dear to other people or which are indeed the object of absolutely held values and sentiments. I suppose this ultimate licence is the greatest when the people who exercise it—being guardians of precious things—are in a position to do great damage.

Related to the licence to think relatively about dear things and absolute values is the licence to do dangerous things. I refer not to the danger run by the steeple-jack and by the men who navigate submarines, for that is danger merely to themselves. (Even so there is a certain disposition to pay these people off with a licence to run slightly amok when the one comes down and the other up to solid ground.) I speak rather of the licence of the physician to cut and dose, of the priest to play with men's salvation, of the scientist to split atoms; or simply the danger that advice given a person may be wrong, or that work done may be unsuccessful or cause damage.

Such licence appears to be as chronically suspect as it is universal in occurrence. In the hearts of many laymen there burns a certain aggressive suspicion of all professionals, whether plumbers or physicians. In some people it flares up into raging and fanatical anger. There are angry people who have or believe that they have suffered injury from incompetent or careless professionals or that they have been exploited by being acted upon more for the professional's increase of knowledge, power, or income, than for the client's own well-being. Many anti-vivisectionists, according to Helen MacGill Hughes, are not those who love beasts more, but those who love physicians less, suspecting them of loving some parts of their work too much.[1] Occasionally such anger spreads as a popular reaction. Nowadays some professions have engaged public relations people to eradicate not merely the more open manifestations of suspicion and anger against them, but to root out deeper and perhaps more chronic feelings of suspicion of laymen against those who have licence to perform services for them. It is but natural that, our culture being what it is, professionals should be disturbed at not being utterly liked; on the other hand, the effort to destroy that last minim of suspicion may precipitate a new suspicion, that of the legitimacy of the public relations man himself. That suspicion may in turn bring renewed suspicion of those who engage public relations men to influence public attitudes toward them.

Herein lies the whole question of the nature of the bargain between those who receive a service and those who give it, and of the circumstances in which it is protested by either party. Of even greater sociological import is the problem of general questioning of licences or mandates. Social unrest often shows itself precisely in questioning of the prerogatives of the leading professions. In time of crisis, there may arise a general demand for more complete conformity of professionals to lay modes of thought, discourse and action.

One of the major professional deviations of mind, a form of guilty knowledge, is the objective and relative attitude mentioned above. One order of relativity has to do with time; the professional may see the present in longer perspective than does the layman. The present may be, for him, more crucial in that it is seen as a link in a causative chain of events; the consequences of present action may appear to

1. "The Compleat Anti-vivisectionist," *The Scientific Monthly*, Vol. LXV, No. 6 (Dec. 1947), pp. 503-7.

him as more inevitable, rippling down through time. The emergency, from this perspective, may appear greater to the professional than to the layman. In another sense, it may appear less crucial, since the professional sees the present situation in comparison with others; it is not unique. Hence the emergency is not so great as the affected layman may see it.

Something like this seems to lie under the attack upon the Supreme Court following its recent decisions upon civil rights; and upon professors who insist on freedom to discuss all things in this time of Cold War. They are thought to be fiddling legal and academic tunes while the Communists are burning the city of freedom. We may any moment now expect similar attack upon those who teach Greek poetry and philosophy while Sputniks are whirling in outer space. In time of crisis, detachment appears the most perilous deviation of all, the one least to be tolerated. The professional mind, in such a case, appears as a perversion of the common sense of what is urgent and what less urgent. The licence to think in longer perspective thus may appear dangerous.

Militant religious sects give us an instructive case. They ordinarily, in Christianity at least, consist of people who are convinced that they are all in imminent danger of damnation. So long as they remain militant sects they are in chronic crisis. They consequently usually do not tolerate a professional clergy or much differentiation of spiritual function at all. It is as if they sense that the professionalizing of spiritual, as of other functions, inevitably brings some detachment, some relativity of attitude, some tendency to compare even the things of the soul. In a large society the clergy may generally be more ardent than most elements of the laity; a sect might almost be defined as a religious group in which the opposite is true. Inquisitions to the contrary, it is probable that professional clergy tend to be more tolerant than the more ardent among the laymen. While it may seem paradoxical to suggest it, one may seriously ask under what circumstances religious people tolerate a professional clergy.

The typical reform movement is a restless attempt of laymen to redefine values, or at least to change the nature and tempo of action about some matter over which an occupational group, or several occupations, holds a mandate. The movement may simply push for faster or more drastic action where the profession is moving slowly or not at all; it may be direct attack upon the dominant philosophy of the profes--sion, as in some attempts to change the manner of distributing medical care. The power of an occupation to protect its licence and to maintain its mandate, the circumstances in which they are attacked, lost or changed; all these are matters for investigation. Such investigation is study of politics in the very fundamental sense of studying constitutions. For constitutions are the fundamental relations between the effective estates which make up the body politic. In our society some occupations are among the groups which most closely resemble what were once known as estates. While there has been a good deal of study of the political activities of occupational groups, the subject has been somewhat misunderstood as a result of the strong fiction of political neutrality in our society. Of course, a certain licence to be politically neutral has been allowed some occupations; but the very circumstances and limits of such neutrality are a matter for study. Special attention should be given the exchanges implied and the circumstances, some of which have been mentioned, in which licence is denied, and the ways in which it is violated and subverted from within and from without. A later chapter will present some data concerning the political neutrality of official statisticians—a group of professionals who consider themselves especially outside the political battle.

I have not in these pages by any means exhausted consideration of the very many variations of licence and mandate and of the relations between them. School teachers in our society, as individuals, have but little licence to think thoughts which others don't think; they aren't even supposed to think the nastier thoughts that others do think. They have almost a negative licence in this regard, in that they are expected in many communities to be rather innocuous, although not heroic, examples to the young. Their mandate seems to be limited to defining matters of pedagogy and is strongly questioned even on that point. There are many people nowadays who would like a return to some previous form of pedagogy which they think superior to what they think is the prevailing method now. Certainly the teaching profession is not succeeding in this country in winning a mandate to say what things children shall be taught. Educational policy is given into their hands but grudgingly. On the other hand, they have a great deal more licence in the handling of children than people believe, by a sort of default. The ability of laymen to see just what goes on in a professional relationship involving the things and people dear to them is always somewhat limited. Durkheim referred to something which he called the impermeability of professions to outside view and intervention.[2]

The educational profession also has a certain mandate by default, in addition to that which they have won by action and propaganda. The lay public in this, as in other matters, by its very lack of persistent and informed concern, leaves in the hands of professionals much of the definition of philosophy, law and action, with respect to a vital concern.

The notions of licence and mandate could be applied to study of the underworld and of social deviation in general, and to the study of artists and entertainers. The people of the underworld have a considerable licence to deviate from ordinary norms of conduct; in fact, they get their living by helping respectable people escape these norms. But the licence of the underworld is never quite admitted. The way

2. *Op. cit.*

in which they find spokesmen and the nature of the exchanges between them and the more respectable world have often been discussed as a pathology of politics. The full circle of exchanges, with all their implications, has not been analyzed with an eye to learning something fundamental about the very nature of social exchanges and hence about the nature of society itself. Study of the licence of artists and entertainers can also yield much knowledge concerning the degrees of conformity in society and the consequences of trying to reduce deviation to something like zero. For these occupations seem to require, if they are to produce the very things for which society will give them a living of sorts (or, in some cases, unheard of opulence), at least some people who deviate widely from the norms more or less espoused and adhered to by other people. Their licence, however, is periodically in a parlous state, and there seems to be no guarantee that it will not at any moment be attacked. On the other hand, it seems never permanently to be withdrawn.

These remarks about licence, mandate and the moral division of labor are meant to introduce rather than to be a definitive analysis. They suggest one of the lines along which investigation about occupations becomes investigation of the nature of society itself.

7

Mistakes at Work

THE COMPARATIVE STUDENT of man's work learns about doctors by studying plumbers; and about prostitutes by studying psychiatrists. This is not to suggest any degree of similarity greater than chance expectation between the members of these pairs, but simply to indicate that the student starts with the assumption that all kinds of work belong in the same series, regardless of their places in prestige or ethical ratings. In order to learn, however, one must find a frame of reference applicable to all cases without regard to such ratings. To this end, we seek for the common themes in human work. One such theme is that of routine and emergency. By this I mean that one man's routine of work is made up of the emergencies of other people. In this respect, the pairs of occupations named above do perhaps have some rather close similarities. Both the physician and the plumber do practice esoteric techniques for the benefit of people in distress. The psychiatrist and the prostitute must both take care not to become too personally involved with clients who come to them with rather intimate problems. I believe that in the study of work, as in that of other human activities and institutions, progress is apt to be commensurate with our ability

The Canadian Journal of Economics and Political Science. Vol. XVII, (August, 1951), pp. 320-27. Reprinted with permission.

to draw a wide range of pertinent cases into view. The wider the range, the more we need a fundamental frame of reference.

Another theme in human work is the problem of mistakes and failures. It, too, is found in all occupations. The more times per day a man does a given operation, the greater his chance of doing it wrong sometimes. True, his skill may become so great that his percentage of errors is nearly zero. It is common talk in the medical profession that certain surgical operations really ought not to be done at all, except *in extremis*, by men who do not have the opportunity to do them literally by the hundreds every year. In a large and favorably known hospital, the interns and residents—who are there to learn by practice—complain that the leading members of the surgical staff take all the interesting cases, not merely out of charity, but to keep their level of skill up to the point of least risk for the few patients who can pay a really high fee. This reduces the opportunities of the interns and residents to acquire skill. One may speak of a calculus of the probability of making mistakes, in which the variables are skill and frequency of performance. It is obvious that there are many possibilities. One who never performs a given action will never do it wrong. But one who has never tried it could not do it right if he were on some occasion compelled to try. This is the position of the layman with reference to many skills. Some skills require more repetition than others for the original learning and for maintenance. In some, even the most proficient make many failures, while in others the top level of skill is close to perfection. Occupations, considered as bundles of skills, are subject to the contingencies contained in all combinations of these factors of learning and of maintaining skill, and, correlatively, subject to variations in the probability that one will sometimes make mistakes. These are matters in which experimental and vocational psychologists are much interested and on which they are doing significant work.

But there are other factors in this problem of mistakes and failures. Some mistakes are more fateful than others, either for the person who makes them, for his colleagues, or for the persons upon whom the mistakes are made. Those who train students for research which requires receiving the confidences of living people and getting and keeping entrée to groups and institutions of various sorts are aware of this problem. (We are at present working on a project to discover how to train students to a high level of skill in social observation with the least risk of damage to all concerned.) In occupations in which mistakes are fateful and in which repetition on living or valuable material is necessary to learn the skills, it is obvious that there is a special set of problems of apprenticeship and of access to the situations in which the learning may be done. Later on, when the neophyte is at his work, there arises the problem of his seeming always to have known how, since the very appearance of being a learner is frightening. At any rate, there are psychological, physical, social, and economic risks in learning and doing one's work. And since the theoretical probability of making an error some day is increased by the very frequency of the operations by which one makes one's living, it becomes natural to build up some rationale to carry one through. It is also to be expected that those who are subject to the same work risks will compose a collective rationale which they whistle to one another to keep up their courage, and that they will build up collective defenses against the lay world. These rationales and defenses contain a logic that is somewhat like that of insurance, in that they tend to spread the risk psychologically (by saying that it might happen to anyone), morally, and financially. A study of these risk-spreading devices is an essential part of comparative study of occupations. They have a counterpart in the devices which the individual finds for shifting some of the sense of guilt from his own shoulders to those of the larger company of his colleagues. Perhaps this is the basis of the strong identification with colleagues in work in which mistakes are fateful, and in which even long training and a sense of high calling do not prevent errors.

Now let us approach the subject from the side of the person who, since he receives the services, will suffer from the mistakes when they are made. In a certain sense, we actually hire people to make our mistakes for us. The division of labor in society is not merely, as is often suggested, technical. It is also psychological and moral. We delegate certain things to other people, not merely because we cannot do them, but because we do not wish to run the risk of error. The guilt of failure would be too great. Perhaps one reason why physicians do work gratis for each other's families is to keep completely free from the economic necessity of treating people with whom they are so closely involved that mistakes would be too hard to face.

Sometimes a person requires an assurance that can be had only by being in a strictly lay frame of mind. Belief in the charism of skill is a lay, rather than a professional, attitude. The professional attitude is essentially statistical; it deals in probabilities. But there are matters about which we prefer to think in absolutes. In dealing with such matters we delegate the relative way of thinking to another, who becomes our agent. He runs our risks for us. We like to believe him endowed with charism. Ray Gold, who studied some of the building trades, found that the housewife likes to believe that the plumber she calls in is perfect, not merely *relatively* good. He keeps the mysterious entrails of her precious house in order. How much more does one want to believe absolutely in one's dentist, lawyer, physician, and priest. (There are of course other non-technical factors involved in delegation of tasks. Some work is *infra dignitate*. Some is necessary, but shady, or forbidden by one's particular taboos and aversions.)

Now this does not mean that the person who delegates
work, and hence, risk, will calmly accept the mistakes which
are made upon him, his family, or his property. He is quick
to accuse; and if people are in this respect as psychiatrists
say they are in others, the more determined they are to escape
responsibility, the quicker they may be to accuse others for
real or supposed mistakes.

In fact, I suppose that we all suspect just a little the ob-
jectivity of those to whom we delegate the more fateful of
our problems. We suspect them for that very experimental
spirit which we know is, in some degree, necessary to hardy
and progressive skill in meeting our crises. Thus there is
probably always some ambivalence in our feelings towards
the people whom we hire to make our mistakes, or at least
to run the risk of making them. The whole problem or set
of problems involved in delegating work—and risks—to
others is one on which there is not much to be found in the
anthropological, sociological, or psychological literature. For
each occupation that one studies one should, I believe, seek
to determine just what it is that is delegated to the persons
in the occupation and what are the attitudes and feelings
involved on both sides.

We now have before us the problem and the characters.
The characters are the people who, because they do something often and for others, run the risk of making mistakes
and of causing injury; and those other people who, for technical, economic, psychological, moral, or status reasons, delegate some of their tasks and problems to others and who therefore may have mistakes made upon them and at their expense.
These are not really two kinds of people, but are the same
people in different roles. The relation of these two roles is
part of the personal adjustment of everyone who works. The
problem is the reduction and absorption of the risk of failure
on both sides, and of the kinds of conflicts within and between

persons, which arise from the risk of error, mistakes, and failures.

As soon as we go into these problems we are faced with another: that of defining what a failure or mistake is in any given line of work or in a given work operation. This leads to still another, which turns out to be the significant one for the social drama of work: Who has the right to say what a mistake or a failure is? The findings on this point are fairly clear; a colleague-group (the people who consider themselves subject to the same work risks) will stubbornly defend its own right to define mistakes, and to say in the given case whether one has been made.[1] Howard S. Becker has found that professional jazz musicians will do considerable injury to themselves rather than let any layman, even the one who is paying their wages, say that a musician is playing badly or even that he has struck the wrong note. An orchestra leader who would even relay a layman's complaint to a member of his band would be thought already on the road to becoming a "square," one of those outsiders who do not understand jazz music. Now you may say that jazz music is so lacking in any canons of correctness that there is no such thing as a single false note within the larger noise. It is all a matter of individual opinion. There is no clear and objective standard by which a judgment can be made.

But how clear is it in other lines of work? When one starts comparing occupations in this regard one finds that in most of them it is very difficult to establish criteria of success or failure, and of mistakes as against proper execution of

1. The colleague-group does not in all cases succeed in getting and keeping this right. Perhaps they do not always want the full responsibility of convicting one another of error and of applying sanctions. It would be more correct to say that a kind of jurisprudence of mistakes is an essential part of the study of any occupation. Professor Norman Ward has suggested that a study of the official *error* in baseball would throw light on the processes involved.

work. The cases where all parties to the work drama would agree are few indeed. In factories which make precision parts the criteria are finely measured tolerances, but usually there is an informally agreed upon set of tolerances which are slightly looser than those in the book. Workmen and inspectors are continually at odds over the difference, even when the workmen want the parts they make to be workable. This is a case of the clearest kind of criterion. In medicine the criteria of success and failure are often far from clear. Dr. Bruno Bettelheim recently stated that psychotherapists do not discuss together their successes and failures because there are no standards to go by; that is why, he said, they spend so much time discussing whether their historical reconstructions of the troubles of their patients are correct or not. Health is, after all, a relative matter. Most people are interested in making the old body do as long as possible; this makes medicine quite a different matter from the automobile industry (where the garage man makes his work easier by persuading you the old car isn't worth mending).

Even where the standards may be a little clearer than in medicine and education, the people who work and those who receive the product as goods or services will have quite different degrees and kinds of knowledge of the probabilities and contingencies involved. The colleague-group will consider that it alone fully understands the technical contingencies, and that it should therefore be given the sole right to say when a mistake has been made. The layman, they may contend, cannot even at best fully understand the contingencies. This attitude may be extended to complete silence concerning mistakes of a member of the colleague-group, because the very discussion before a larger audience may imply the right of the layman to make a judgment; and it is the *right* to make the judgment that is most jealously guarded.

In some occupations it is assumed that anyone on the

inside will know by subtle gestures when his colleagues believe a mistake has been made. Full membership in the
colleague-group is not attained until these gestures and their
meaning are known. When they are known, there need not
be conscious and overt discussion of certain errors even
within the colleague-group. And when some incident makes
an alleged failure or mistake a matter of public discussion,
it is perhaps the feeling that outsiders will never understand
the full context of risk and contingency that makes colleagues
so tight-lipped. And if matters have gone to such a point
that mistakes and failures are not freely discussed even within
the trusted in-group, public discussion may be doubly feared;
for in addition to questioning the prerogative of in-group
judgment, the outside inquisitor lifts the veil from the group's
own hidden anxieties, the things colleagues do not talk about
even among themselves. This may be the source of the rather
nervous behavior of school teachers when my colleagues
and I report to them—at their own request—some of the
things we are finding out about them.

One of the differences between lay and professional
thinking concerning mistakes is that to the layman the technique of the occupation should be pure instrument, pure
means to an end, while to the people who practice it, every
occupation tends to become an art. David Riesman,[2] who
was once a clerk to Justice Brandeis, and an assistant in the
office of the District Attorney of New York, tells of the wonderful briefs which young lawyers draw up for presentation
to lower court judges who can scarcely read them, much
less judge the law that is in them. The ritual of looking up
all the past cases, and the art of arguing out all possibilities
are gone through, even when the lawyer knows that the decision will be made upon a much simpler—perhaps also a

2. "Toward an Anthropological Science of Law and the Legal Profession," *The American Journal of Sociology*, LVII (September, 1951), pp.
121-35.

much sounder—basis. What is more: the ritual and the art are respected, and the men who perform them with brilliance and finesse are admired. The simple client may be dazzled, but at some point he is also likely to think that he is being done by the whole guild of lawyers, including his own, the opposing counsel, and the court. In a sense, the art and cult of the law are being maintained at his expense. The legal profession believes, in some measure, in the cult of the law. The individual case is thought of not merely as something to be decided, but as part of the stream of observance of the cult of the law.

And here we come to the deeper point of Dr. Bettelheim's remark concerning his own colleagues, the psychotherapists. A part of their art is the reconstruction of the history of the patient's illness. This may have some instrumental value, but the value put upon it by the practitioners is of another order. The psychotherapists, perhaps just because the standards of cure are so uncertain, apparently find reassurance in being adept at their art of reconstruction (no doubt accompanied by faith that skill in the art will bring good to patients in the long run).

Another example of these ways of thinking is to be found in social work. This profession is said to make a distinction between successful and professional handling of a case. The layman thinks of success as getting the person back on his feet, or out of his trouble. The social worker has to think of correct procedure, of law, of precedent, of the case as something which leaves a record. She also appreciates skilful interviewing, and perhaps can chuckle over some case which was handled with subtlety and finish, although the person never got "well" (whatever that would be in social work).

In teaching, where ends are very ill-defined—and consequently mistakes are equally so—where the lay world is quick to criticize and blame, correct handling becomes ritual as much as or even more than an art. If a teacher can prove that he has followed the ritual, the blame is shifted from himself to the miserable child or student; the failure can be and is put upon them.

Ritual is also strongly developed in occupations where there are great unavoidable risks, as in medicine. In such occupations the ritual may, however, be stronger in the second and third ranks of the institutions in which the work is done. Thus, in medicine, the physician, who stands at the top of the hierarchy, takes the great and final risks of decision and action. These risks are delegated to him, and he is given moral and legal protection in taking them. But the pharmacist, who measures out the prescribed doses, and the nurse, who carries out the ordered treatment, are the great observers of ritual in medicine. Pharmacists are said often to become ritualistic wipers and polishers, flecking infinitely small grains of dust from scales on which they are only going to weigh out two pounds of Paris green. The ritualistic punctiliousness of nurses and pharmacists is a kind of built-in shock-absorber against the possible mistakes of the physician. Indeed, in dramatizing their work, these second-rank professions explicitly emphasize their role as saviors of both patient and physician from the errors of the latter. And here again we get a hint of what may be the deeper function of the art, cult, and ritual of various occupations. They may provide a set of emotional and even organizational checks and balances against both the subjective and the objective risks of the trade.

I suspect that it is a rare occupation whose practitioners develop no criteria of good work, and no concept of mistake or failure other than simply defined successful conclusion of the given case or task. Usually the professional judgment will contain explicit or implicit references to an art, a cult, and a ritual. The function of the art, cult, and ritual is not so much to bring the individual case to an early successful conclusion as to relate it to the on-going occupation itself, and to the social system in which the work is done. In most occupations, a man can be judged as quite wrong by his colleagues for an action which the lay client might consider very successful indeed. The quack, defined functionally and not in evaluative terms, is the man who continues through time to please his customers but not his colleagues. On the contrary, a man may be considered by his colleagues to have done a piece of work properly and without error, even when the client may accuse him of error, mistake, or failure.

In this remarks I have mentioned two concepts of great importance for study of the universal work drama. One is the concept of role; the other, that of social system. A person, asked what his work is, can answer in two ways. He can say *what* he does: I make beds, I plumb teeth. Or he can say *who* he is: I am the person who does so and so. In the latter case he is naming his role. A large part of the business of protecting one's self from the risks of one's own work mistakes lies in definition of role; and in some occupations, one of the rewards is definition of one's role in such a way as to show that one helps protect people from the mistakes of others. Now, roles imply a system of social arrangements. Most work is done in such systems. Part of the function of these systems is to delegate, to spread, or, in some cases, to concentrate, the risk and the guilt of mistakes; and also to spread and to allocate the losses which result from them. The details of these matters are better left until they have been worked out more fully.

This one example of sociological analysis prompts some remarks concerning the academic division of labor with reference to human work. In the historical and conventional division of academic labor, work has belonged to the economists, as do voters and kings to the political scientist, and fun and vice to the sociologist. The historian handled anything which had been written down on paper or other material long enough ago for the author, his characters, and all the relatives of both to be so long dead that no one would bring a libel suit. Indeed, it was better if they were in danger of being forgotten, for the historian's fame depended on re-discovering them. But his mandate allowed him to tell all about his characters—their work, their politics, and their gambols. The anthropologist went about the earth on one-man expeditions discovering people who didn't write and hadn't been written about. Since he was alone in the field and since his reputation depended upon his being the first there, he looked at everything from hair texture and the shape of shin bones to religion, art, kinship, crime, and even the technique and organization of work, and the distribution of the products of labor.

Now the division of academic labor, like other human arrangements, is as much the result of social movements as of logic. Some persons in, or on the periphery of, academic life are seized, from time to time, with a new preoccupation. They pursue it and their successors nourish it. The third generation will have refined out of it some pure essence which will be called a social science; but they will not ordinarily have yielded to anyone else the original liquor from which their essence was distilled. Thus, the pure essence of economic reasoning was abstracted from preoccupation with all sorts of things having to do with the material and moral welfare of man, as may be seen in Adam Smith's *The Wealth of Nations*. Since the quantities which would appear in place of the letters in economic equations—if some economist were to be so impure as to make such a substitution—would include the price of the labor used in manufacturing and distributing those goods which are produced in sufficient quantities to fit the formulae, it is quite natural that work should have been one of the preoccupations of the economist. Indeed, it was natural that economists should extend their interest to whatever might affect the price and supply of labor: migration, the birth-rate, religion and philosophy, laws, trade unions, politics, and even mental and physical capacities, although the latter have become the psychologists' claim to entry into the factory. Economists have been interested in those distractions from labor which have more lately been the concern of the sociologist, but which Daniel Defoe, who never heard of sociology, commented upon in *The True-Born Englishman*:

> The lab'ring poor, in spight of double pay
> Are sawcy, mutinous and beggarly
> So lavish of their money and their time
> That want of forecast is the nation's crime
> Good drunken company is their delight
> And what they get by day, they spend by night.

If the occupation of the economist be economic reasoning, in ever more sophisticated formulae, human work continues to be one of his *pre*occupations. And this illustrates the fate of each branch of social science; that while it refines and purifies its theoretical core, its logic, it can never free itself from the human mess. Wallowing there, each purist will find himself in the company of others who, although they seek to create a different pure product of logic, must extract it from this same mess. It might be of some use, in these days of the cult of collaboration between the social disciplines, for us to understand the social movements out of which the various social sciences have come, and the consequent development in each not merely of a central and distinguishing logic, but of a large periphery or halo of preoccupation with institutions and events. It is, I believe, treading upon a pre-empted area of events and institutions that brings accusation of academic trespass, rather than borrowing its fundamental logic. Thus a sociologist should stay out of factories because the economist was there first. The economist should stay out of the family. Neither of them should be caught in an insane asylum, which is the domain of psychiatrists.

But, to the extent that there is some logic in the academic division of labor, representatives of each discipline will be found studying not merely some one institution but any events which yield to effective analysis by their particular logic. Economics will cease to be merely—if it ever was—the science of markets; anthropology, of primitive peoples; education, of what happens in schools; sociology, of families, churches, playgrounds, settlement houses, and prisons.

Human work, including the institutions in which people work for a living, has become one of the lively frontiers on which social scientists meet. Without belaboring the point, I refer you to V. W. Bladen for an acute analysis of what is happening among economists, anthropologists, and sociologists on this frontier.[3] Work, I submit, is in all human societies an object of moral rule, of social control in the broadest sense, and it is precisely all the processes involved in the definition and enforcement of moral rule that form the core problems of sociology.

---

3. "Economics and Human Relations," *The Canadian Journal of Economics and Political Science,* Vol. 14 (August, 1948), pp. 301-11.

8

Dilemmas and
Contradictions of Status

IT IS DOUBTFUL whether any society ever had so great a variety of statuses or recognized such a large number of status-determining characteristics as does ours. The combinations of the latter are, of course, times over more numerous than the characteristics themselves. In societies where statuses* are well defined and are entered chiefly by birth or a few well-established sequences of training or achievement, the particular personal attributes proper to each status are woven into a whole. They are not thought of as separate entities. Even in our society, certain statuses have developed characteristic patterns of expected personal attributes and a way of life. To such, in the German language, is applied the term *Stand*.

Few of the positions in our society, however, have remained fixed long enough for such an elaboration to occur.

The American Journal of Sociology. Vol L (March, 1945), pp. 353-59. Reprinted with permission.

* "Status" is here taken in its strict sense as a defined social position for whose incumbents there are defined rights, limitations of rights, and duties. See the *Oxford Dictionary* and any standard Latin lexicon. Since statuses tend to form a hierarchy, the term itself has—since Roman times— had the additional meaning of rank.

We put emphasis on change in the system of positions which make up our social organization and upon mobility of the individual by achievement. In the struggle for achievement, individual traits of the person stand out as separate entities. And they occur in peculiar combinations which make for confusion, contradictions, and dilemmas of status.

I shall, in this paper, elaborate the notion of contradictions and dilemmas of status. Illustrations will be taken from professional and other occupational positions. The idea was put into a suggestive phrase by Robert E. Park[1] when he wrote of the "marginal man." He applied the term to a special kind of case—the racial hybrid—who, as a consequence of the fact that races have become defined as status groups, finds himself in a status dilemma.

Now there may be, for a given status or social position, one or more specifically determining characteristics of the person. Some of them are formal, or even legal. No one, for example, has the status of physician unless he be duly licensed. A foreman is not such until appointed by proper authority. The heavy soprano is not a prima donna in more than temperament until formally cast for the part by the director of the opera. For each of these particular positions there is also an expected technical competence. Neither the formal nor the technical qualifications are, in all cases, so clear. Many statuses, such as membership in a social class, are not determined in a formal way. Other statuses are ill-defined both as to the characteristics which determine identification with them and as to their duties and rights.

There tends to grow up about a status, in addition to its specifically determining traits, a complex of auxiliary characteristics which come to be expected of its incumbents. It seems entirely natural to Roman Catholics that all priests

---

1. Park, Robert E., "Human Migration and the Marginal Man," *American Journal of Sociology*, Vol. XXXIII (May, 1928), pp. 881-93. Also in Park, Robert E., *Race and Culture*. Glencoe (Ill.), 1950.

should be men, although piety seems more common among women. In this case the expectation is supported by formal rule. Most doctors, engineers, lawyers, professors, managers, and supervisors in industrial plants are men, although no law requires that they be so. If one takes a series of characteristics, other than medical skill and a licence to practice it, which individuals in our society may have, and then thinks of physicians possessing them in various combinations, it becomes apparent that some of the combinations seem more natural and are more acceptable than others to the great body of potential patients. Thus a white, male, Protestant physician of old American stock and of a family of at least moderate social standing would be acceptable to patients of almost any social category in this country. To be sure, a Catholic might prefer a physician of his own faith for reasons of spiritual comfort. A few ardent feminists, a few race-conscious Negroes, a few militant sectarians, might follow their principles to the extent of seeking a physician of their own category. On the other hand, patients who identify themselves with the "old stock" may, in an emergency, take the first physician who turns up.[2]

If the case is serious, patients may seek a specialist of some strange or disliked social category, letting the reputation for special skill override other traits. The line may be crossed also when some physician acquires such renown

2. A Negro physician, driving through northern Indiana, came upon a crowd standing around a man just badly injured in a road accident. The physician tended the man and followed the ambulance which took him to the hospital. The hospital authorities tried to prevent the physician from entering the hospital for even long enough to report to staff physicians what he had done for the patient. The same physician, in answer to a Sunday phone call asking him to visit a supposedly very sick woman, went to a house. When the person who answered the door saw that the physician was a Negro, she insisted that they had not called for a doctor and that no one in the house was sick. When he insisted on being paid, the people in the house did so, thereby revealing their lie. In the first instance, an apparently hostile crowd accepted the Negro as a physician because of urgency. In the second, he was refused presumably because the emergency was not great enough.

that his office becomes something of a shrine, a place of wonderful, last-resort cures. Even the color line is not a complete bar to such a reputation. On the contrary, it may add piquancy to the treatment of a particularly enjoyed malady or lend hope to the quest for a cure of an "incurable" ailment. Allowing for such exceptions, it remains probably true that the white, male, Protestant physician of old American stock, although he may easily fail to get a clientele at all, is categorically acceptable to a greater variety of patients than is he who departs, in one or more particulars, from this type.

It is more exact to say that, if one were to imagine patients of the various possible combinations of these same characteristics (race, sex, religion, ethnic background, family standing), such a physician could treat patients of any of the resulting categories without a feeling by the physician, patient, or the surrounding social circle that the situation was unusual or shocking. One has only to make a sixteen-box table showing physicians of the possible combinations of race (white and Negro) and sex with patients of the possible combinations to see that the white male is the only resulting kind of physician to whom patients of all the kinds are completely accessible in our society (see Table 1).

One might apply a similar analysis to situations involving other positions, such as the foreman and the worker, the teacher and the pupil. Each case may be complicated by adding other categories of persons with whom the person of the given position has to deal. The teacher, in practice, has dealings not only with pupils but with parents, school boards, other public functionaries, and, finally, his own colleagues. Immediately one tries to make this analysis, it becomes clear that a characteristic which might not interfere with some of the situations of a given position may interfere with others.

I do not maintain that any considerable proportion of

people do consciously put together in a systematic way their expectations of persons of given positions. I suggest, rather, that people carry in their minds a set of expectations concerning the auxiliary traits properly associated with many of the specific positions available in our society. These expectations appear as advantages or disadvantages to persons who, in keeping with American social belief and practice, aspire to positions new to persons of their kind.

The expected or "natural" combinations of auxiliary characteristics become embodied in the stereotypes of ordinary talk, cartoons, fiction, the radio, and the motion picture. Thus, the American Catholic priest, according to a popular stereotype, is Irish, athletic, and a good sort who with difficulty refrains from profanity in the presence of evil and who may punch someone in the nose if the work of the Lord demands it. Nothing could be farther from the French or French-Canadian stereotype of the good priest. The surgeon, as he appears in advertisements for insurance and pharmaceutical products, is handsome, socially poised, and young of face but gray about the temples. These public, or publicity, stereotypes—while they do not necessarily correspond to the facts or determine people's expectations—are at least significant in that they rarely let the person in the given position have any strikes against him. Positively, they represent someone's ideal conception; negatively, they take care not to shock, astonish, or put doubts into the mind of a public whose confidence is sought.

If we think especially of occupational status, it is in the colleague-group or fellow-worker group that the expectations concerning appropriate auxiliary characteristics are worked most intricately into sentiment and conduct. They become, in fact, the basis of the colleague-group's definition of its common interests, of its informal code, and of selection of those who become the inner fraternity—three aspects of occupational life so closely related that few people separate them in thought or talk.

The epithets "hen doctor," "boy wonder," "bright young men," and "brain trust" express the hostility of colleagues to persons who deviate from the expected type. The members of a colleague-group have a common interest in the whole configuration of things which control the number of potential candidates for their occupation. Colleagues, be it remembered, are also competitors. A rational demonstration that an individual's chances for continued success are not jeopardized by an extension of the recruiting field for the position he has or hopes to attain, or by some short-cutting of usual lines of promotion, does not, as a rule, liquidate the fear and hostility aroused by such a case. Oswald Hall found that physicians do not like one of their number to become a consultant too soon.[3] Consulting is something for the crowning, easing-off years of a career; something to intervene

Table 1[4]

PATIENT	PHYSICIAN			
	White Male	White Female	Negro Male	Negro Female
White Male	....	....	....	....
White Female	....	....	....	....
Negro Male	....	....	....	....
Negro Female	....	....	....	....

briefly between high power and high blood-pressure. He who pushes for such practice too early shows an "aggressiveness" which is almost certain to be punished. It is a threat to an order of things which physicians—at least, those of the

3. Hall, Oswald. "The Informal Organization of Medical Practice." Unpublished Ph.D. dissertation. University of Chicago, 1944. ———, "The Stages of a Medical Career," *The American Journal of Sociology*, LIII, (March 1948), pp. 327-36.

4. Cf. Williams, Josephine J., "Patients and Prejudice; Lay Attitudes toward Women Physicians," *The American Journal of Sociology*, LI (Jan. 1946), pp. 283-87.

fraternity of successful men—count upon. Many of the specific rules of the game of an occupation become comprehensible only when viewed as the almost instinctive attempts of a group of people to cushion themselves against the hazards of their careers. The advent of colleague-competitors of some new and peculiar type, or by some new route, is likely to arouse anxieties. For one thing, one cannot be quite sure how "new people"—new in kind—will act in the various contingencies which arise to test the solidarity of the group.[5]

How the expectations of which we are thinking become embodied in codes may be illustrated by the dilemma of a young woman who became a member of that virile profession, engineering. The designer of an airplane is expected to go up on the maiden flight of the first plane built according to the design. He (*sic*) then gives a dinner to the engineers and workmen who worked on the new plane. The dinner is naturally a stag party. The young woman in question designed a plane. Her co-workers urged her not to take the risk—for which, presumably, men only are fit—of the maiden voyage. They were, in effect, asking her to be a lady rather than an engineer. She chose to be an engineer. She then gave the party and paid for it like a man. After food and the first round of toasts, she left like a lady.

Part of the working code of a position is discretion; it allows the colleagues to exchange confidences concerning their relations to other people. Among these confidences one finds expressions of cynicism concerning their mission, their competence, and the foibles of their superiors, themselves, their clients, their subordinates, and the public at large. Such expressions take the burden from one's shoulders and serve as a defense as well. The unspoken mutual confidence necessary

---

5. It may be that those whose positions are insecure and whose hopes for the higher goals are already fading express more violent hostility to "new people." Even if so, it must be remembered that those who are secure and successful have the power to exclude or check the careers of such people by merely failing to notice them.

to them rests on two assumptions concerning one's fellows. The first is that the colleague will not misunderstand; the second is that he will not repeat to uninitiated ears. To be sure that a new fellow will not misunderstand requires a sparring match of social gestures. The zealot who turns the sparring match into a real battle, who takes a friendly initiation too seriously, is not likely to be trusted with the lighter sort of comment on one's work or with doubts and misgivings; nor can he learn those parts of the working code which are communicated only by hint and gesture. He is not to be trusted, for, though he is not fit for stratagems, he is suspected of being prone to treason. In order that men may communicate freely and confidentially, they must be able to take a good deal of each other's sentiments for granted. They must feel easy about their silences as well as about their utterances. These factors conspire to make colleagues, with a large body of unspoken understandings, uncomfortable in the presence of what they consider odd kinds of fellows. The person who is the first of his kind to attain a certain status is often not drawn into the informal brotherhood in which experiences are exchanged, competence built up, and the formal code elaborated and enforced. He thus remains forever a marginal man.

Now it is a necessary consequence of the high degree of individual mobility in America that there should be large numbers of people of new kinds turning up in various positions. In spite of this and in spite of American heterogeneity, this remains a white, Anglo-Saxon, male, Protestant culture in many respects. These are the expected characteristics for many favored statuses and positions. When we speak of racial, religious, sex, and ethnic prejudices, we generally assume that people with these favored qualities are not the objects thereof. In the stereotyped prejudices concerning others, there is usually contained the assumption that these other people are peculiarly adapted to the particular places which they have held up to the present time; it is a corollary implication that they are not quite fit for new positions to which they may aspire. In general, advance of a new group—women, Negroes, some ethnic groups, etc.—to a new level of positions is not accompanied by complete disappearance of such stereotypes but only by some modification of them. Thus, in Quebec the idea that French-Canadians were good only for unskilled industrial work was followed by the notion that they were especially good at certain kinds of skilled work but were not fit to repair machines or to supervise the work of others. In this series of modifications the structure of qualities expected for the most-favored positions remains intact. But the forces which make for mobility continue to create marginal people on new frontiers.

Technical changes also break up configurations of expected status characteristics by altering the occupations about which they grow up. A new machine or a new managerial device—such as the assembly line—may create new positions or break old ones up into numbers of new ones. The length of training may be changed thereby and, with it, the whole traditional method of forming the person to the social demands of a colleague-group. Thus, a snip of a girl is trained in a few weeks to be a "machinist" on a practically foolproof lathe; thereby the old foolproof machinist, who was initiated slowly into the skills and attitudes of the trade, is himself made a fool of in his own eyes or—worse—in the eyes of his wife, who hears that a neighbor's daughter is a machinist who makes nearly as much money as he. The new positions created by technical changes may, for a time, lack definition as a status. Both the technical and the auxiliary qualifications may be slow in taking form. The personnel man offers a good example. His title is perhaps twenty years old, but the expectations concerning his qualities and functions are still in flux.[6]

6. The personnel man also illustrates another problem which I do not propose to discuss in this paper. It is that of an essential contradiction be-

Suppose we leave aside the problems which arise from technical changes, as such, and devote the rest of this discussion to the consequences of the appearance of new kinds of people in established positions. Every such occurrence produces, in some measure, a status contradiction. It may also create a status dilemma for the individual concerned and for other people who have to deal with him.

The most striking illustration in our society is offered by the Negro who qualifies for one of the traditional professions. Membership in the Negro race, as defined in American mores and/or law, may be called a master status-determining trait. It tends to overpower, in most crucial situations, any other characteristics which might run counter to it. But professional standing is also a powerful characteristic—most so in the specific relationships of professional practice, less so in the general intercourse of people. In the person of the professionally qualified Negro these two powerful characteristics clash. The dilemma, for those whites who meet such a person, is that of having to choose whether to treat him as a Negro or as a member of his profession.

The white person in need of professional services, especially medical, might allow him to act as doctor in an emergency. Or it may be allowed that a Negro physician is endowed with some uncanny skill. In either case, the white client of ordinary American social views would probably avoid any nonprofessional contacts with the Negro physician.[7] In fact,

---

tween the various functions which are united in one position. The personnel man is expected to communicate the mind of the workers to management and then to interpret management to the workers. This is a difficult assignment. The problem is well stated by William F. Whyte, in "Pity the Personnel Man," *Advanced Management*, October-December, 1944, pp. 154-58. The Webbs analyzed the similar dilemma of the official of a successful trade-union in their *History of Trade-Unionism* (rev. ed.; London: Longmans, Green, 1920).

7. The Negro artist can be treated as a celebrity. It is within the code of social tufthunting that one may entertain, with a kind of affected Bohemian intimacy, celebrities who, on all counts other than their artistic accomplishments, would be beyond the pale.

one way of reducing status conflict is to keep the relationship formal and specific. This is best done by walking through a door into a place designed for the specific relationship, a door which can be firmly closed when one leaves. A common scene in fiction depicts a lady of degree seeking, veiled and alone, the address of the fortuneteller or the midwife of doubtful practice in an obscure corner of the city. The anonymity of certain sections of cities allows people to seek specialized services, legitimate but embarassing as well as illegitimate, from persons with whom they would not want to be seen by members of their own social circle.

Some professional situations lend themselves more than others to such quarantine. The family physician and the pediatrician cannot be so easily isolated as some other specialists. Certain legal services can be sought indirectly by being delegated to some queer and unacceptable person by the family lawyer. At the other extreme is school teaching, which is done in full view of the community and is generally expected to be accompanied by an active role in community activities. The teacher, unlike the lawyer, is expected to be an example to her charges.

For the white colleagues of the Negro professional man the dilemma is even more severe. The colleague-group is ideally a brotherhood; to have within it people who cannot, given one's other attitudes, be accepted as brothers is very uncomfortable. Furthermore, professional men are much more sensitive than they like to admit about the company in which nonprofessionals see them. The dilemma arises from the fact that, while it is bad for the profession to let laymen see rifts in their ranks, it may be bad for the individual to be associated in the eyes of his actual or potential patients with persons, even colleagues, of so despised a group as the Negro. The favored way of avoiding the dilemma is to shun contacts with the Negro professional. The white physician or surgeon of assured reputation may solve the problem by acting as consultant to Negro colleagues in Negro clinics and hospitals.

For the Negro professional man there is also a dilemma. If he accepts the role of Negro to the extent of appearing content with less than full equality and intimacy with his white colleagues, for the sake of such security and advantage as can be so got, he himself and others may accuse him of sacrificing his race. Given the tendency of whites to say that any Negro who rises to a special position is an exception, there is a strong temptation for such a Negro to seek advantage by fostering the idea that he is unlike others of his race. The devil who specializes in this temptation is a very insinuating fellow; he keeps a mailing list of "marginal men" of all kinds and origins. Incidentally, one of the by-products of American mores is the heavy moral burden which this temptation puts upon the host of Americans who have by great effort risen from (*sic*) groups which are the objects of prejudice.

There may be cases in which the appearance in a position of one or a few individuals of a kind not expected there immediately dissolves the auxiliary expectations which make him appear odd. This is not, however, the usual consequence. The expectations usually continue to exist, with modifications and with exceptions allowed.

A common solution is some elaboration of social segregation. The woman lawyer may become a lawyer to women clients, or she may specialize in some kind of legal service in keeping with woman's role as guardian of the home and of morals. Women physicians may find a place in those specialities of which only women and children have need. A female electrical engineer was urged by the dean of the school from which she had just been graduated to accept a job whose function was to give the "woman's angle" to design of household electrical appliances. The Negro professional man finds his clients among Negroes. The Negro sociologist generally studies race relations and teaches in a Negro college. A new figure on the American scene is the Negro personnel man in industries which have started employing Negro workers. His functions are to adjust difficulties of Negro workers, settle minor clashes between the races, and to interpret management's policies to the Negro as well as to present and explain the Negro's point of view to management. It is a difficult job. Our interest for the moment, however, is in the fact that the Negro, promoted to this position, acts only with reference to Negro employees. Many industries have had women personnel officials to act with reference to women. In one sense, this is an extension of the earlier and still existing practice of hiring from among a new ethnic group in industry a "straw boss" to look after them. The "straw boss" is the liaison officer reduced to lowest terms.

Another solution, which also results in a kind of isolation if not in segregation, is that of putting the new people in the library or laboratory, where they get the prestige of research people but are out of the way of patients and the public. Recently, industries have hired a good many Negro chemists to work in their testing and research laboratories. The chemist has few contacts with the production organization. Promotion within the laboratory will put the Negro in charge of relatively few people, and those few will be of his own profession. Such positions do not ordinarily lead to the positions of corresponding importance in the production organization. They offer a career line apart from the main streams of promotion to power and prestige.

These solutions reduce the force of status contradiction by keeping the new person apart from the most troublesome situations. One of the consequences is that it adds new stories to the superstructure of segregation. The Negro hospital and medical school are the formal side of this. The Negro personnel man and foreman show it within the structure of existing institutions. There are evidences that physicians of various ethnic groups are being drawn into a separate medical system of hospitals, clinics, and schools, partly because of the interest of the Roman Catholic Church in developing separate institutions but also partly because of the factors here discussed. It is doubtful whether women will develop corresponding separate systems to any great extent. In all of these cases, it looks as if the highest point which a member of these odd groups may attain is determined largely by the number of people of his own group who are in a position to seek his services or in a position such that he may be assigned by other authority to act professionally with reference to them. On the other hand, the kind of segregation involved may lead professional people, or others advanced to special positions, to seek—as compensation—monopoly over such functions with reference to their own group.

Many questions are raised by the order of things here discussed. One is that of the place of these common solutions of status conflict in the evolution of the relations between the sexes, the races, and the ethnic groups of our society. In what circumstances can the person who is accepted formally into a new status, and then informally kept within the limits of the kind mentioned, step out of these limits and become simply a lawyer, foreman, or whatever? Under what circumstances, if ever, is the "hen doctor" simply a doctor? And who are the first to accept her as such—her colleagues or her patients? Will the growth of a separate superstructure over each of the segregated bottom groups of our society tend to perpetuate indefinitely the racial and ethnic division already existing, or will these superstructures lose their identity in the general organization of society? These are the larger questions.

The purpose of the paper, however, is not to answer these large questions. It is rather to call attention to this characteristic phenomenon of our heretogeneous and changing society and to suggest that it become part of the frame of reference of those who are observing special parts of the American social structure.

9

The Making of a Physician

SOCIAL SCIENTISTS are being called upon more and more to study training for the various professions and to consult with those who make policy with reference to it. The following pages suggest a general frame of reference for such study. They were written for several people, both medical educators and social scientists, who were thinking of embarking on a modest study tracing the course of students through the maze of a particular medical school. There resulted a day-long discussion which was of great value in planning the study. It was more like a prolonged group interview than a formal discussion. While the ideas refer specifically to medicine, they implicitly refer to other professions as well.

THE MEDICAL CULTURE

Each of the great historic professions is concerned with not just a set of techniques for doing some useful work, but with some aspect of life and/or society, itself. And when, as often happens, an occupation—either an old one transformed by technical or social changes, or a new one—claims for itself the status of profession, it is saying to the world that—like

Human Organization. Vol. 14 (Winter, 1955), pp. 21-25. Reprinted with permission.

the professions—the work it does has somehow become a matter of broad public concern.

Medicine is the prototype of the professions in this regard. As Sigerist so well demonstrates in the first chapter of his work,[1] a history of medicine is a history of human society and culture, of its metaphysics as well as of its physics, of its basic philosophy of nature, of its ideas of health and disease, of the processes of therapy (faith, magic, science, and arts), and its notions about the proper economy and distribution of goods and services, including healing services and facilities.

These ideas, the health and illness aspect of a culture, are never the sole possession and certainly never the exclusive creation of those who devote themselves to the healing arts. On the other hand, the medical culture of the dominant healing profession (or professions, for they are not so united in all as in our own culture) never coincides exactly with that of the lay world. The relations between professional medical culture and lay medical culture have varied a great deal; in our part of the world, most of the population accepts the basic assumptions of the former. This is still not so in many parts of the world; and where it is not, the medical profession faces special problems. But even in our world the lay public, or parts of it in varying degree, does not accept all the assumptions, nor the therapeutic and preventive measures based upon them. Furthermore, the accumulation of medical knowledge and art has become so great that those without special training are, perhaps, relatively further from the professional in relevant knowledge and skill than in earlier periods. In a sense, we are more dependent upon the professionals for medical services than were our ancestors. By the same token, only some small portion of medical knowledge and skill can be mastered by each member of the profession itself, which leads

1. Henry E. Sigerist, *A History of Medicine,* Vol. 1, *Primitive and Archaic Medicine,* New York, 1951, "Introduction," pp. 3-101.

to there being subcultures within the greater professional medical culture. This is also more than a matter of technique and knowledge; it has roots in ideas and assumptions. One can, with some truth, speak of the medical philosophy, perhaps even of the moral, social, or economic philosophy of the various specialties; one can at least speak of differences of emphasis among them. Some of the specialties may even be said to have their own lay publics—people who accept their basic philosophy and who favor their approach to diagnosis and treatment rather than others.

Medical culture goes far beyond these approaches. For one thing, an approach to health may carry implications about the relations of physicians to each other, about the degrees of cooperation necessary and/or desirable among them. For another, from the very nature of their work, physicians cannot refrain from having opinions about the relations of physicians to patients, to the public, and to the many other occupations, enterprises and institutions involved in health activities. Professionals and laymen might accept the same assumptions about the nature of disease and its treatment, yet differ strongly on the proper relations of the various parties involved. Indeed, among both laity and the profession there are differences on many of these points which may or may not be related to specialties, differences in social, ethnic, or regional background and so on.

However these things may be, it is beyond dispute that there is an immense and elaborate medical culture in our world, and that the knowledge and attitudes that make it up are distributed in various ways among laity and the medical profession and related occupations.

MEDICAL EDUCATION

Medical education is the whole series of processes by which the medical culture is kept alive (which means more than merely imparted) through time and generations, by which it is extended to new populations or elements of the population, and by which it is added to through new learning and experiment. The education of the medical profession is part of it. For our immediate purposes we will use the phrase medical education only for the training and initiation of physicians, although there is a certain danger of distortion in using it in so limited a way. The education of the members of the medical profession is a set of planned and unplanned experiences by which laymen, usually young and acquainted with the prevailing lay medical culture, become possessed of some part of the technical and scientific medical culture of the professionals. The starting point is the lay medical culture; the end point varies, although the learning experiences are somewhat standardized and although all must take standard examinations to be licensed. But the end point is not there, for in varying ways and degrees the professionals must bring what they have learned into effective interaction with the lay medical culture again. But with a difference—for they themselves are in a new role.

Part of the medical culture of the lay world is some set of conceptions about the proper role of the physician and a set of beliefs about the extent to which he lives up to the role so conceived, and the extent to which and the ways in which he falls short. Initiation into a new role is as much a part of medical training as is the learning of techniques; indeed, part of it is to learn the techniques of playing the role well. A role is always a part in some system of interaction of human beings; it is always played opposite other roles. To play one is not to play another. One might say that the learning of the medical role consists of a separation, almost an alienation, of the student from the lay medical world; a passing through the mirror so that one looks out on the world from behind it, and sees things as in mirror writing. In all of the more esoteric occupations we have studied we find the sense of seeing the world in reverse.

The period of initiation into the role appears to be one wherein the two cultures, lay and professional, interact within the individual. Such interaction undoubtedly goes on all through life, but it seems to be more lively—more exciting and uncomfortable, more self-conscious and yet perhaps more deeply unconscious—in the period of learning and initiation. To take one example, the layman has to learn to live with the uncertainty if not of ignorance, at least of lack of technical knowledge of his own illnesses; the physician has to live with and act in spite of the more closely calculated uncertainty that comes with knowing the limits of medical knowledge and his own skill.

In the process of change from one role to another there are occasions when other people expect one to play the new role before one feels completely identified with it or competent to carry it out; there are others in which one overidentifies oneself with the role, but is not accepted in it by others. These and other possible positions between roles make of an individual what is called a marginal man; either he or other people or both do not quite know to what role (identity, reference group) to refer him. We need studies which will discover the course of passage from the laymen's estate to that of the professional, with attention to the crises and the dilemmas of role which arise.

Stereotype and reality.—We assume that anyone embarking upon the road to medicine has some set of ideas about what the work (skills and tasks) of the physician is, about what the role is, what the various medical careers are, and about himself as a person who may learn the skills, play the role, and follow one of the possible career-lines. We assume also that except in cases of extraordinary early contact with the profession, the medical aspirant's conceptions of all these things are somewhat simpler than the reality, that they may be somewhat distorted and stereotyped as among lay people. Medical education becomes, then, the learning of the more complicated reality on all these fronts. It may turn out that it makes a good deal of difference whether the steps toward a more penetrating and sophisticated reality on one of these points come early or late, and whether the reality is learned from supporting teachers and colleagues or rubbed in by punishing cynics or stubborn and uncomprehending patients. It may be that the more complicated reality is in some circumstances traumatic, in others, exciting and even inspiring. Perhaps some aspects of reality can be learned in an early phase of technical training and experience, while others can be effectively learned only at some later point. There has always been considerable talk in educational institutions about what kinds of things are prerequisites for others; only in a few cases does it appear really to be known what should come first, what later—there are those who say that geometry should come before algebra, not after. Some question the time-honored custom of having students learn anatomy from cadavers rather than from demonstrations with living persons. In the study of professional education, we have suggested a distinction between various kinds of prerequisites: conventional and symbolic, technical and role-learning. Learning the realities of medical skills, roles and careers may move *pari passu;* or it may be that some of the roles can be really learned only when a certain level of skill has been attained and certain career corners turned. The realities about career problems might at some points put a damper on the student's eagerness to learn skills and roles; at another point, a new knowledge of career realities might be a stimulus to work on the other fronts.

In professional, as in other lines of work, there grows up both inside and outside some conception of what the essential work of the occupation is or should be. In any occupation, people perform a variety of tasks, some of them approaching more closely the ideal or symbolic work of the profession than others. Some tasks are considered nuisances and impositions, or even dirty work—physically, socially or morally beneath the dignity of the profession. Part of what goes on with respect to a major aspect of life at whose center is a profession, such as the medical, is a constant sorting and resorting of the tasks involved among many kinds of people—inside the profession, in related professions, and clear outside professional ranks. The preparation of drugs, the taking of blood pressures, the giving of anaesthetics, the keeping of medical records, the collection of bills, the cleaning up of operating rooms, the administration of hospitals—these are but a few of the tasks which have been allocated and reallocated within the medical division of labor in fairly recent years. There is constant discussion of what is whose work in medicine and what part of it all is the physician's work, privilege and duty. We assume that the medical student is inducted into the discussion of these problems, and that it has some effect upon his motivation and his sense of mission. We may suppose that the essential, symbolically-valued part of the physician's work is diagnosis and treatment of the ailments of people, and that the other activities are—in theory at least—tolerated only as they appear necessary to it. What, then, are considered essential auxiliary or peripheral activities, and what attitudes do physicians hold toward them and the people who perform them? Hospitals must be administered, and there are some who believe that physicians alone should do it. Yet, physicians do not ordinarily gain great prestige by becoming administrators—indeed, some who are say they are scarcely considered medical colleagues any longer. On the other hand, there is some tendency for auxiliary activities to become valued ends in themselves, sometimes even getting in the way of the presumed basic activity (as discipline becomes an end in itself in schools and, some say, in nursing).

The increasing variety of the central and, symbolically, most valued of medical activities themselves is reflected in the number of medical specialties. Some of the specialties are rated above others both by laymen and the profession, although these ratings are not necessarily the same. We may assume that as the student learns various skills and sees at closer hand the actual tasks of his future trade, he will undergo changes of attitude toward them as components of medical work.

Just as certain tasks and skills of medical work are rated above others, so also are the men who perform them. But we must remember that the various medical tasks differ from each other not merely in the knowledge and technical skill required, but in the social relations and social roles involved. The model member of the profession is a man of certain skills and knowledge, one who keeps proper balance between the more and the less valued activities of the profession, and who plays his role well in relation to himself, his colleagues, other personnel in medical work, and toward his patients and the public. As in other professions, we may find that some models are—like the saints—considered a little too good for ordinary men to be expected to imitate in daily practice, although they are admired as embodiments of the highest values of the profession. A study of medical education should discover not merely the saintly models, but also those the student regards as more practically (even a bit cynically) attainable by himself, the mold being as it is, and he being who he is. The shift in choice of models by the student, his definite steps or his drifting into the path that leads to one model rather than others, is a significant part of his medical education. This is, of course, not merely choice of specialty, but of various ways of practicing medicine: practice, teaching, research; practice in one social environment rather than another: rural or urban, well-off or poor, where the health standard of living is high or is low, among his own or among other kinds of people; alone or in association with others; for salary or for fees; where competition is keen or where there is more security, etc. These matters may all enter as components into models to be admired or followed, which is to say that, as suggested above, a model in effect embodies the whole professional ideology of those who choose it.

The models of the medical world are, of course, not free of influence from the ideologies of other aspects of modern life. We should investigate the extent to which the image of the model businessman has colored that of the model physician. Although the world of business uses the term *private entrepreneur* there is plenty of evidence that the model businessman is seen as a team worker rather than a person who goes it alone. It is possible that in some respects the medical model is a hangover from the outmoded one of the business world. Given current trends in medical organization, it seems obviously important to discover not merely the extent to which the go-it-alone model prevails as against the team-work model, but also to find out what influences continue to reinforce it.

The conception of the model physician contains, by implication, clues to the nature of the model patient. There may be a good deal of ambivalence on this point, since few students are so unrealistic as to believe they can get a practice consisting of only one kind of patient (as to troubles, personal, social, or economic characteristics), or so divinely endowed and blissfully ambitious that they can in fact get such a clientele. It is recognized, too, that all people must be served in some fashion. Yet there are conceptions of the ideal patient: about what is wrong with him, about his social and economic characteristics, about his acceptance of the physician's authority and prescriptions, his understanding, his co-operation and his gratitude. There are apparently at least three important components in these conceptions: the nature of the illness and its amenability to treatment; the nature of the interaction between the patient in his role with the physician in his; and, finally, the effect of the patient on the physician's career (income, reputation, development of further skill, fulfillment of his self-concept as a physician).

We have said little directly about the nature of social roles, and will make only a few remarks on the subject since, by implication, the problem of role is found throughout. In one sense, a role is what a man expects of himself and what others expect of him in certain situations. People sometimes expect miracles of physicians; the physician has to learn how to handle this expectation in such a way as to give his patients both the best chance of getting well and the least chance of disillusionment. This is the eternal problem of helping people to face uncertainty, or unwelcome certainty (as the case may be), the problem of maintaining balance in the relations between the more skilled partner (the physician) and the less skilled, but more crucially-affected partner (the patient). Man of understanding, man of patience, confidante, advisor, pillar of strength—and their opposites—these are terms having to do with roles, rather than with techniques as such.

They all involve other people, or oneself considered in one's relations to other people. Everyone has to work out the weights he will give to the various parties to the work drama in which he has a role. Will he play it for the patients alone, dramatizing himself as their champion against the profession itself? Taken to the extreme, this is quackery in a strict sociological sense, whether or not the man be competent in his methods of diagnosis and practice. There are people who play their roles before their colleagues alone, or before some of their colleagues rather than others; still others may be moved by peculiar conceptions of their own rights and duties, impervious alike to colleague and patient. These may be the true missionaries, the sectarians who have no judge except God himself. Every man finds his "significant others," with whom he identifies himself so that he listens to their voices rather than to others. This is what is meant by the recently-adopted term, "reference group." Since there are a number of crucial reference groups in modern medicine, it becomes part of the problem of the student to find some balance between his sensitivity to them, his own configuration of significant others. Different configurations may be associated with selection of the specialties and the ways of practicing mentioned above.

It is also likely that as he goes through his medical education, the aspirant will veer from one toward another of his significant others; at one time feeling the aches and pains of the patient more acutely than the patients themselves; at another sharing the angry cynicism of those colleagues who say, in their hour of disillusion with ungrateful humanity, that the only thing to do is get yours while you can; at another, feeling the exhilaration of wonder-working, and yielding a bit to the blandishments of admiring nurses, students, and grateful patients; and at still another, suffering the pangs of uncertainty of his trade and feeling sorry for himself.

This leads to the problem of self-conception and discovery of self. A person's conception of himself is itself something of a stereotype, to which parents, teachers, siblings, peers, and his own dreams have contributed. Some people project themselves far into the future, others operate more or less in the present. But in either case, there come moments of necessary revision and adjustment of one's notions about what he can do and wants to do. One may say, then, that a young man thinking about himself as a physician is thinking about a young man as yet somewhat unknown to himself, doing work and playing roles not yet known, in situations he has never yet been in. This is not to underestimate the anticipatory playing of roles; but no matter how sensitive the individual's anticipation of himself in a future role, there is some gap between anticipation and realization. Certainly, there are more young men in premedical school who think of themselves as potential surgeons than can ever be surgeons, given the qualities necessary and the proportion of the medical profession who make their living as such. There are also fewer who expect to end up in public health than actually will. As he proceeds through medical training and into practice, the young man may be expected to get not merely a better notion of the skills required, of the tasks to be performed, of the roles to be played, and of the positions to be attained in the medical world and the roads which lead toward them, but also to adjust his conception of his own mental, physical and personal aptitudes, his tastes and distastes, and of the chances that a person of his particular social and economic qualities and family circumstances may acquire the skills, the roles and the positions available.

This is an economics of self-conception. The importance of this to the distribution of physicians among specialties and ways of practicing is obvious. Again we have to deal with the problems of fateful or crucial choice. A person may make a discovery about himself only after he has passed the point of crucial decision to do the kind of work he would now like to have been able to do. In the concrete, this means that one cannot enter medicine at all unless one has had certain schooling by a certain age; that some specialties have to be adopted far earlier than others; that some require a longer period of doing without income; that a wife who is a handicap in one kind of practice might be a great asset in another; that, while one can master the skills of a certain specialty, one has no taste or aptness for the social roles required. A study of the progressive self-discovery of students passing through the maze of medical school and training might be used by those who plan the experiences which have a bearing on the choice of effective models, of specialties, and of the ways and places of practice by medical students.

Career. One of the problems in the study of a profession

is to discover the career-lines of people who follow it. This in turn requires identification of the significant phases of careers, and the sequences in which they occur. Sequences occur in all the matters we have discussed thus far. Some of them are institutionalized—as the sequence from premedical phase, to medical student, to intern, resident, practicing physician, diplomate of a specialty body, etc. Others are not so formally institutionalized and named, but are well known. Still others are more or less unnoticed or not admitted (but nevertheless often anticipated or feared) regularities of change from one ill-defined phase to another. One changes from a young man with teachers and mentors to whom he may turn, into an older man who has become a teacher and a sponsor, even a father-figure to younger men. Or one finds that one has less time for the clinic and the laboratory because of the increase of administrative demands upon one's time. One aspect of career is just these shifts from one weighting or combination of activities to another. It is well known that these shifts are accompanied by anxieties, such as shown in the dream of a young woman who had just been made a supervisor of nursing in a large hospital. She dreamed that she suddenly had to get a patient into a respirator at night, and that she had either forgotten how, or else a new model had been brought in—and she fumbled while the patient gasped. The shift from one kind of activity to another entails the danger of losing a skill; it is also a shift from one kind of responsibility to another, from one role to another.

There are, in any kind of career line, points of negative and positive crucial decision. For example, if I have not received my specialty residence in a certain kind of hospital by a certain age, certain further steps are closed. There is also always before a young man the question whether, when, and how often to move from one place of work to another. Some lines of work, and some specialties within medicine, show different patterns of relation between moving and success. One would expect that the career of a man going into private practice might be more crucially affected by his first choice of a place to practice than is the career of a man who goes in for pathology, teaching, or any of the specialties in which work for salary is the rule. There is, in institutions or systems, a certain balance between home-guard success and itinerant success. The home-guard are the people who make their careers with little or no itineracy; the itinerants progress by moving from one place or institution to another. Those who get ahead by moving—from say, smaller to larger schools or hospitals—have to decide whether to move in a small orbit (state or region) or in a large, perhaps national or international, orbit. The decision, or the fact—whether it be by conscious decision or by default—of operating in a small or in a large orbit involves the choice of significant others (reference groups), the people on whose good opinion one stakes one's reputation; those whom one can afford to pay less attention to; and those, perhaps, from whom one must dissociate oneself. It involves, in short, the choice of his closer colleagues, the people who will refer cases to him, the people who will think of him when they want a teammate, the people who see his potentialities and help him to realize them.

Career is, in fact, a sort of running adjustment between a man and the various facts of life and of his professional world. It involves the running of risks, for his career is his ultimate enterprise, his laying of his bets on his one and only life. It contains a set of projections of himself into the future, and a set of predictions about the course of events in the medical world itself. Much is to be learned about career lines, how they are conceived by the students of medicine and how their personal and social backgrounds, school and other training experiences, predispose or turn them in one or another of the many directions in which a medical man may go. It is the sum total of these dispositions and turnings that gives us the kind of distribution of physicians we have among the various ways of practicing and the various places and settings within which medicine is practiced, whether that distribution be good or poor.

We are in a time of great change in the institutions of medicine. Not only is their inner structure changing so that the available positions and careers and the demands made upon those who fill them are in flux both in number and kind, but there are more and more ancillary institutions, more and more connections of medicine with the other concerns and institutions of the world. The younger physician's projection of himself into the future is consequently a projection with more unknowns in it than ever before. The whole trend of the system itself is something of an unknown. So that the problem becomes in part that of adjusting to running, never-completed adjustment. Some will doubtless accept the implications of such open-endedness more than others; some may indeed make it part of their identity to be men who do not seek a fixed identity, men whose constant is that they are open to change, or even men who seek the spots where change is the major assignment. Others may seek, successfully or not, the spots which appear most fixed, the bastions that appear safe from storming. We may find a home-guard of time, as well as of space.

We need studies which will run these various lines of inquiry concurrently, starting in the premedical phase and following the aspirant through into his early years of practice. That is, studies which take him from the time when he is most nearly like a layman in his medical culture, through the full cycle of whatever happens to him in school, to that time in the early years of practice when he is fully a member of the profession, both in his own mind and in that of most people who know him.

10

Professions in Transition

THE OCCUPATIONS historically known as professions are undergoing great changes in the organization of their work. Medicine, in response to changes in both medical technology and philosophy, has been broken up into many specialties. There has also been a phenomenal increase in the equipment used in diagnosis and treatment of patients. One result has been concentration of the bulky and expensive equipment, of the physicians themselves, and of many other kinds of help into great clinics and hospitals. The patients now come to the equipment and the physician. This, in turn, has brought drastic changes in the physician's relations to his colleagues, his patients, and also makes it necessary for him to deal with many new kinds of medical workers; the contingencies of his career are now, in large part, those of his relations to institutions.

The client of the lawyer is more and more often an organization—a limited liability company, an association, a government bureau; less often an individual. To serve rich and huge corporate clients lawyers have been gathered into large

---

This chapter is based somewhat on "Discussion of the Bryan Report," in Asheim, Lester (ed.), *A Forum on the Public Library Inquiry* (New York, 1950), pp. 106-14.

firms where each man can specialize in some line of law. The lawyer who practices alone in a large American city is, indeed, a lawyer in name only; he does little of the legal reasoning and of the skillful arguing which are considered true law work. The young lawyer goes, more and more often, directly from law school to a firm which pays him a salary; he has a single employer instead of many clients.

The professions, although they are prospering under these changes, are made uneasy by them. For in these historic professions—the free professions, as they are called in German— the individual practitioner is supposed to stand in a fiduciary relation which he must scrupulously keep clean of interests which arise out of his relation to other clients. The current trends appear to endanger this supposedly simple relation of professional with client. Oddly enough, however, just at this moment of transition in the organization of their practice, the professions apparently enjoy a prestige greater than ever before. Furthermore, it is a time of trend toward professionalism, according to the most important article of recent years on the place of professions in society, "The Recent History of Professionalism in Relation to Social Structure and Social Policy," by T. H. Marshall.[1] He refers to the fact that a good many services formerly carried out in an informal way by amateurs are now performed by specialists who work in large private or public organizations. They require people of high literary and technical training, and whose quality of effort can be trusted. For while, says Marshall, *caveat emptor* may make some sense when one buys goods which he can see in advance, it is utter nonsense in relation to services which one can never see in advance. A. M. Carr-Saunders and P. A. Wilson,[2] writing of the same trend, have shown the steps which

---

1. T. H. Marshall, "The Recent History of Professionalism in Relation to Social Structure and Social Policy," *The Canadian Journal of Economics and Political Science,* V (August, 1939), pp. 325-34.

2. A. M. Carr-Saunders and P. A. Wilson, *The Professions* (Oxford, 1933).

an occupation goes through in trying to establish itself as a profession.

And this is the second sense in which this is a time of professions in transition: The practitioners of many occupations—some new, some old—are self-consciously attempting to achieve recognition as professionals. Among them are librarians, social workers, and nurses. As long as there have been libraries, there have been people who kept them, but the librarian that we now know is a product of the proliferation of public and other libraries which seek to circulate rather than merely to hoard books. The sick apparently have always been nursed, but nursing as we know it is something still taking form in the modern hospital and public health agency; Florence Nightingale is already obsolete, except as a symbolic founding mother. Assistance and counsel have always been given to those in trouble, but social work, too, is a newcomer and a striver among the professions. All these occupations, in their present form, result from new technical development, social movements and/or new social institutions. The old service or function, formerly performed by amateurs or for pay by people of little or no formal training, comes to be the lifework of a large and increasing number of people. Its basic techniques are changed. Most of the new professions, or would-be professions, are practised only in connection with an institution. Their story is thus that of the founding, proliferation or transformation of some category of institutions: schools, social agencies, hospitals, libraries, and many others. Whether the institution be new or whether it be an old one transformed, there is likely to be a struggle of the new profession with the other occupations involved (if there are any), and with the laymen who have some voice in the institution—a struggle for definition of the part of each in the functioning of the institution.

At first, the people who are recruited to the occupation come, of necessity, from other occupations. If they are women, many of them may have had no previous gainful occupation. They will be of various social backgrounds, ages, and kinds of education. Some are more amateur than professional. In time, the question of training arises. The first people to take formal training, when schools for the purpose are established, are likely to be people already at work in the occupation. As time goes on, the occupation and its training schools become better known, and young people are recruited at the same age as for other schools. The training school itself generally starts as a vocational school, without college or university connections and with terms of study that do not correspond to the academic calendar. The early teachers are enthusiastic leaders of a movement, or protagonists of some new technique (such as case work), who have little conventional academic training and who find their colleagues in the new movement rather than in the academic world. They, or some leader among them, institute a curriculum which is likely to persist for some time and to be thought so sacred that to propose to alter it drastically is considered heretical.

In time, the training schools may seek and gain connection with universities, some of which compete for students and for the prestige and money accorded the new profession. At this point, there may be a new wave of later seekers of special training; as in nursing, where a whole generation of leaders sought academic degrees some years after having completed their nonacademic professional training.

The development continues in the direction of standard terms of study, academic degrees, eventually higher degrees, research in some field or fields considered proper to the profession and the institution in which it operates, and a continuing corps of people who teach rather than practice the profession directly. At the same time, prerequisites to the professional training will be multiplied, with the result— intended or not—of requiring candidates for the occupation to decide earlier to enter training, and to make a "firm commitment." By increasing the length of the training, the time and social cost of leaving training, once it is started, becomes greater. The standardized schooling and training become, in the successful case, effectively the licence to work at the occupation.

These developments inevitably bring a campaign to separate the sheep from the goats, to set up categories of truly professional and of less-than-professional people. This takes time, because many people in the occupation do not have the full new training, and because those who have power of appointment to places do not fully accept the occupational group's right to say who can be hired for the work. The professional group will go through a process of self-consciously studying its work and deciding what functions are really professional and what can be delegated to nonprofessional or less-than-professional people. Nurses are delegating much of their former work to practical nurses, aides, and maids, while continually taking on new duties assigned to them by physicians and the administrators of hospitals. The librarians are in a campaign to rid themselves of purely clerical work, so that they may follow their true work, that of advising people about what to read. So far as this sorting out of functions is successful, it has a double effect. Some functions are down-graded: bed-making and housekeeping for nurses; the dusting, handling, chasing, cataloguing, date-stamping of books for librarians; "means test" interviewing for social workers. The people who do them are also down-graded, or else a new category of non-professional or less-than-professional people is introduced into the system to perform these *infra dignitate* tasks. This development has been especially marked in nursing, aided by a shortage of help in hospitals. It is just now being talked of in teaching, where it is proposed that there should be master teachers who do naught but teach, while others counsel pupils, correct papers, and keep discipline.

Even among those who qualify as fully professional, some

will be swept more completely than others into the main stream of change and professionalization. Some will have drifted into the occupation, and will not want to leave home to take new jobs. Others, more fully committed and more alert to the new developments will move from place to place seeking ever more interesting, prestigeful and perhaps, more profitable positions. The latter become itinerants, interchangeable parts in the larger system of things, at home in any given place not because of personal attachments, but because of the work to be done and the conditions of doing it. Those who stay longer in one place, whether because they have no opportunity to move, or because they have attachments, build even more attachments, becoming less movable and perhaps more resistant to the itinerants and the changes the latter propose and promote. The two styles of careers, the home-guard and the itinerant, may show up as a chronic tension in the institutions in which the professionals work, the itinerants as a rule fancying themselves as the more professional, the home-guard perhaps thinking of themselves as having the interests of the home community or institution at heart and fearing that the itinerants may try to relegate them to the limbo of the less-than-professional.

At this point problems of morale and career develop. Shall the people who start in the nonprofessional or less-than-professional auxiliary occupations be kept there, or shall the door be kept ajar for them to get further training and become professionals? This may be an important point of policy for a profession and for institutions faced with recruiting problems. If the decision whether to enter one of the less-than-professional auxiliary trades or the profession itself must be made earlier and irrevocably it can affect both the number and the quality of recruits as well as the relations between the professionals and others at work. It is also likely that if the decision to enter the profession must be made earlier, the number of people who enter for security's sake may increase, while the number of enthusiastic mavericks—so numerous among the founders—will be reduced. This may be happening both in teaching and in nursing, although there are a few experiments being made in the recruiting of bright and well-educated late-choosers.

From all of this there flows the question common to all new professions and by no means uncommon among older ones: for what are the people being trained, anyway? A recent study of librarians gives the impression that the most successful librarian is no longer a librarian, but an administrator (*she* becomes a *he* in the course of it in many cases). This in varying degree is also true of nurses, social workers, and engineers. It has become an acute problem in a number of occupations, although not quite yet in universities, for professors still look down their noses at deans and department chairmen, except when they want some dirty work done, or need money. In a considerable number of professions the basic techniques and intellectual skills are becoming something one learns as a condition of getting on the ladder of mobility. The engineer who, at forty, can still use a slide rule or logarithmic table, and make a true drawing, is a failure. Hence the old remark of condescension mingled with respect: "The old man has forgotten more than you will ever know." It might be that the advanced library schools are merely institutions where people get themselves groomed to stop being librarians and become administrators, just as graduate departments of education are said to serve the purpose of moving people from the little circuits to the big tent circuit in school administration. If the line of promotion in a profession is in the direction of administration, what should the professional training be? And if the professional school becomes a graduate school culminating in a Ph.D.—for which a piece of "research" is required—must one not ask whether this is either the best way to get research done or the best way to train administrators? A piece of research done as part of training for promotion to a position where one will no longer have to do research may probably have some of the faults of a diagnosis done with an eye on what diagnostic procedures the patient can pay for. But we are now talking of problems which may arise in any profession, new or old, when the practice of it becomes involved in complicated institutional settings. The new professions, being so involved from the beginning, may give us some of our best clues for analyzing the problems of the old.

11

Psychology:
Science and/or Profession

LET ME SET BEFORE YOU three occupational models: a science, a business, and a profession. Each of these, in the purest case, shows a system of social interaction different from the others in crucial respects. There are other models, but these appear the most useful ones to those who are discussing the institutional aspect of the occupation of psychology.

Scientists, in the purest case, do not have clients. They discover, systematize, and communicate knowledge about some order of phenomena. They may be guided by a faith that society at large and in the long run will benefit from continued increase of knowledge about nature; but the various actions of the scientist, *qua* scientist, are undertaken because they add to knowledge, not because of any immediate benefit to any individual or group which may be considered his client. The test of the scientists' work lies in convincing communication of it to colleagues, communication so full and

The American Psychologist. Vol. 7 (August, 1952), pp. 441-43. Reprinted with permission. The discussion was written at the request of a committee of the American Psychological Association, appointed to consider a code of ethics for psychologists.

so precise that any of them can undertake to test the validity of claimed findings by following the same procedures. Scientists chafe under secrecy. If laymen do not receive full report of work done, it is simply because they are not sophisticated enough to understand the report. The great point in the scientist's code is full and honest reporting to his colleagues, and, with it, willingness to submit to full criticism. Since this is so, and since no client is involved, scientists ordinarily do not seek the protection of state licence. Informal controls are sufficient.

The second model is that of a business. In purest form, business goes on among traders. Since the customer is also a trader, he is presumed to be as sophisticated about the object traded in as is the seller. The trading is a game. The principle of *caveat emptor* can apply without injury to anyone. As in all games, however, there are rules designed to allow the game to continue. There is no sense letting anyone in who lacks the resources to make good his deals, or the skill to keep the game going. Hence, stock exchanges have limited memberships. But the state and the public are not especially considered in making the rules of entrance to the game and the rules of play.

Not all business is of this pure form, for goods are eventually sold to an amateur, a consumer. The consumer may know what he likes, but he is not expected to be as good a judge of what he buys as is the man who sold it to him. He expects some little protection from unscrupulous sellers who would impose upon his ignorance. *Caveat emptor* tends to be limited, but not completely—witness the tongue-in-cheek "pitch" of advertising. The customer often, in moments of annoyance, initiates action to license sellers or to otherwise protect the customers from them. I introduce this model merely to high-light the third, that of a profession.

The people in a profession make their living by giving an esoteric service. Nowadays it is commonly said that the service is based upon a science or, as in the case of engineering and medicine, a number of sciences. The essence of the matter appears, however, to be that the client is not in a position to judge for himself the quality of the service he receives. He comes to the professional because he has met a problem which he cannot himself handle. It may be a matter of life or death for himself or a loved one; of gaining or losing a family farm, or one's freedom and reputation; of having one's dream of a house turn into wonderful reality or a white elephant. He has some idea of the result he wants; little, of the means or even of the possibility of attaining it. Indeed, he may want an impossible result, and be bitterly resentful of the professional man's judgment that it is impossible. But the time comes when the physician cannot prolong a life. All patients are lost in the long run. Half of all cases contested at law are lost; there is a losing side. All professions fail in some measure to achieve what their clients want, or think they want, of them. Furthermore, members—even the best— of all professions make mistakes of judgment and of technique. The result of all this is that those in the profession do not want the principle of *caveat emptor* to apply. They do not want the client to make an individual judgment about the competence of practitioners or about the quality of work done for him. The interaction between professional and client is such that the professionals strive to keep all serious judgments of competence within the circle of recognized colleagues. A licensing system adds the support of the state to some mechanism established by the profession itself for this purpose. It is as if competence became an attribute of the profession as a whole, rather than of individuals as such. Thus the public is to be protected from its own incompetence and from its own impossible demands, in that "quacks"—who might exploit them—will not be allowed to practice. And the professional, for his part, is protected from his own mistakes and from the allegation that he may have

made one, by the fiction that all licensed professionals are
competent and ethical until found otherwise by their peers.
The profession sets up institutions which make clients' judgments of secondary importance and colleagues' judgments
paramount. These institutions will of necessity require some
arrangements for secret discussion. For it is shocking and pain-
ful to clients to hear their problems discussed as objectively
as must be in deciding whether a professional did, in fact,
show competence and whether he acted in accordance with
the professional code. In such discussion the question of
competence is discussed in complete separation from the out-
come for the client. In protecting the reputation of the profession and the professional from unjust criticism, and in
protecting the client from incompetent members of the profession, secrecy can scarcely be avoided. Secrecy and institutional
sanctions thus arise in the profession as they do not in the
pure science.

I have dwelt upon the professional conception because it
is so highly valued in the western world, and especially in
North America. The people, or some people, in many occupations have sought to have their work conform to the professional model and to be known by the professional name.
Social workers, librarians, and many business occupations
have tried it. The steps taken are much the same in the various
instances. Courses of study are established, and, if possible,
professional schools are founded and attached to universities.
Prerequisites are required so that a person entering the occupation must decide to do so earlier. Eventually some body is
set up to accredit schools and specify the curriculum. Devices
are adopted to define more sharply who is and who is not
properly in the occupation. Canons of proper practice, proper
relations to clients (or employers), proper relations between
colleagues, etc., are set up. Although the steps are essentially
the same, the results vary greatly. The public may not accept
the professional definitions and may continue to take their

troubles to people not admitted to the professional group. Employers may simply hire people without consulting the professional group as to their membership or competence. Shrines and various kinds of irregular practitioners continue through the ages to treat the cases which doctors declare either incurable or imaginary. Sometimes the curriculum of the professional schools may be hardened before the techniques have really been tested in practice or in a laboratory. This happened in social work and in library schools. I do not know whether these things have happened or will do so in psychology. I only point out that they are things which do happen in the course of professionalizing occupations.

It is fairly evident that psychologists are torn between the professional and the scientific conceptions of their work. Only their enemies charge them with pursuit of the business conception. Now medicine has been plagued by this conflict through many years. The marriage between clinic and laboratory is still an uneasy one. The wonder-working surgeon (they do work wonders) is still not quite at ease with the sceptical pathologist down in the laboratory. The practicing physician, meeting as best he can the emergencies of patients who refuse to get made-to-order troubles, feels inferior before his patient and learned brethren of the great research schools and foundations; he also resents their detached, leisurely criticism of his hasty blunders.

The medical solution, at least the one prevailing at present, is to instruct physicians in science but not to train them to be scientific investigators. Any physician who learns to do research in a science related to medicine, does so either in prolonged residencies in research hospitals or by taking advanced work in one or more sciences in a graduate school. There are people who believe that a great deal of the time spent in medical school is wasted, unless it be admitted that sheer initiation into the fraternity is a good way to have young men spend time. However that may be, the medical profession has succeeded in enforcing a highly standardized curriculum upon all who would be called doctors of medicine, no matter what skills and knowledge an individual may use in his particular branch of work. Training in scientific research comes later, for the few who want it. I do not know whether psychology could institutionalize its conflict in such a way. But my point is not so much the particular solution as the fact itself that there is a continuing, deep conflict between the model of science and that of professional practice of medicine. In many individuals, it is an ambivalence.

I suspect that psychology's problem is of this order. I also think it likely that whatever solutions are arrived at will be compromises. They will be better compromises if no one has any illusions about settling the problem once and for all; if it is kept in mind that the conflict lies deep in many occupations, and that all solutions to it are tentative, based on limited time predictions about the effects of various actions.

12

The "Gleichschaltung" of
The German Statistical Yearbook:
A Case in Professional Neutrality

THE VERY SAME ENGINEER, it is said, kept the waterworks of Paris going before, during, and after the French Revolution. The architects of the great cathedrals of the middle ages caricatured bishops and saints in durable stone. Some professions, it seems, have licence to be more politically or ideologically detached than others; freer to hold opinions not those of the prevailing powers, or even—heresy of heresies—to hold no opinion at all on the burning issues of the time. Societies and epochs also quite obviously differ in their demands for conformity; all but the most doctrinaire and totalitarian societies appear to demand more conformity and more commitment from some kinds of people than from others.

The physician is generally thought to have a large measure of licence to be neutral. His magic is wanted alike by believer and infidel. He is supposed to be as impartial as illness and death themselves. His diagnostic and therapeutic decisions are expected to be free of any extraneous influence. A certain

The American Statistician. Vol. IX (Dec., 1955), pp. 8-11.

halo of freedom to be neutral in other things as well as in
his medical judgments seems to gather about his head. Yet
his freedom is neither absolute nor complete. In the Soviet
Union the physician who declares too many people ill enough
to stay away from work may be called to account:[1]

The scarce and indispensable natural scientist may also
be allowed a good deal of political neutrality, although he
too may be questioned not merely about his opinions, but
also about his friends. Social scientists perhaps require more,
but expect less of such freedom. Among them it is perhaps
those who deal exclusively with the numbers and movements
of goods and people who would consider themselves most
neutral. They might also think their jobs—whether they work
in universities or in government bureaus—most safe from
variable high winds of social doctrine, from the coming and
going of parties, and even from the vicissitudes of revolution.
Will not any government need statistical information of un-
questioned reliability in making and executing its policies?

Such thoughts came to my mind when, in the summer of
1953, my eye caught this heading of a table in the *Statistical
Yearbook of the German Reich for 1941-2*: "Racial Classification of People Who Married in 1938." It was the last
such Yearbook published by the National Socialist Government of Adolf Hitler. From earlier work with German official
statistics, I was practically certain that the pre-Nazi German
had had a religion, but not a race. The statistical German was
the opposite of the statistical American, who had a race but no
religion. The accident of noticing this change of categories
in the German census led me to ask a question: What changes
did the statistician of the German Reich have to make in his
official Yearbook when the Nazis came to power? Behind
it lie more general questions for professional statisticians: How
politically neutral is their work? To what extent are the very

1. Field, Mark G., "Structured Strain in the Role of the Soviet Physician," *American Journal of Sociology*. LVIII (March, 1953), pp. 493-502.

categories in which they report their data subject to political demands?

I do not know the answers to these general questions. But I did go through all of the German statistical yearbooks from the last one of the pre-Nazi Weimar Republic, 1932, through the Nazi period, and including the first post-war volume, to see what changes of category and of reporting occurred along with the radical political changes. I don't know how deeply the Nazis dug into the private opinions of the Reich statistician, or whether Party people were put in his office to watch over him. I have only the internal evidence of the Statistical Yearbooks themselves. The last Weimar volume, and all of the Nazi Yearbooks except the last are signed by one Dr. Reichardt of the Reich Statistical Office. The last Nazi volume, 1941-42, is signed Godlewski. Whether Dr. Reichardt simply reached the age of retirement about the end of 1940 or whether he finally turned out to be not sufficiently *gleichgeschaltet* (coordinated), I don't know. Many a man did try to get on with his work by making little compromises, only to find one day that it was impossible to continue and fatal to quit. I must add that I do not know what happened to Godlewski either; he certainly did not sign the first Yearbook of the new Bonn republic.

The Foreword to the last pre-Nazi Yearbook, 1932, is the exact, dull little statement one expects of a faithful public servant who is accustomed to going modestly on with his work while prime ministers and cabinets come and go. It contains no word about parties or government policies. It uses no political symbol. When, in November, 1933, Dr. Reichardt signed the next Yearbook, Hitler had been Reichschancellor for the better part of a year. The Foreword takes no notice of the change. It is the same little businesslike statement about the contents of the book. In the next Foreword, 1934, however, Dr. Reichardt feels called upon to tell the reader that the Yearbook now contains a series of "German economic curves, showing the economic events since the taking over of power by the National Socialist regime." In 1935, the mention becomes a plug, "In the many tables of the Yearbook there come to expression the powerful accomplishments made by the New State in all fields of folk and economic life in the three years since the taking over of power by the National Socialist regime." He especially notes the great success of measures against unemployment. In passing he mentions some new family statistics, and tables on the Special Census of the Occupational and Social Distribution of *Glaubensjuden* (Jews by faith) and Foreigners.

From 1935* on, the Foreword always tells how many years it has been since the National Socialists took power, and reports in more and more glowing terms the accomplishments of the New State. The statement is typically like this, "The Yearbook gives an accounting in sober, but eloquent figures of the measures taken by the New State in all fields of folk and economic life, and the results in population, economics and in cultural and political affairs." Dr. Reichardt even notes that the Yearbook has to be bigger because of the increased activity of the New State. From 1936 on, curves showing economic progress are put on the inside of the front cover where they are the first thing to be seen when one opens the book. In 1938 the flyleaf shows a map entitled "Folk and Space since the Assumption of Power." It shows how the empire has been expanded by the assimilation of Austria and Sudetenland. In 1939-40, a similar map shows most of Western Europe under German "protection." Under the map is a summary table showing the increase of territory and population accomplished by the New State. Dr. Reichardt tells us in his 1938 Foreword that the Yearbook now reports the Greater German Reich; he regrets that not many of the tables take account of the new territories, since comparable statistics do not yet exist. The last two books, done in wartime, no longer bother to plug for the New State. A brief

Foreword says that the Yearbook was produced under difficulties, "because the needs of the State and the Party require it." Readers are enjoined, under penalty, to keep copies in metal safes and to divulge the contents to no one not in government service.

The 1932 Yearbook shows the results of all Reichstag elections from 1919 to 1932, with the number of votes for each party. The most recent election, that of July 31, 1932, was reported in even greater detail. The 1933 book gives the same summary of past elections, and includes the detail of two new elections. One was the election of November, 1932, in which there was a considerable decline of the Nazi vote. In spite of that, Hindenburg had called upon Hitler to form a government. The other was the election of March, 1933, the only free election in the Hitler time; in it the Social Democrats held their own, the Catholic Centre gained a little, and the Nazis gained tremendously. The Communists apparently contributed most to the Nazi increase, since they lost a million votes from November, before Hitler came in, to March, just after he came to power. But this is an aside. The Yearbook merely reports the figures. In 1934 and after, each Yearbook reports only the new-style Yes and No elections of the current year. I do not know whether Dr. Reichardt was told to stop reporting the elections of the late Weimar Republic, or whether he gave it up for purely technical reasons. It would make no sense to try to compare the results of free elections in which a dozen or more parties struggled for slight gains in their popular vote and for more seats in parliament with those of the new style, high-pressure plebiscites in which the choice was to be for or against Hitler. Maybe Dr. Reichardt was not coordinated on this point; it was sufficient that the elections were coordinated.

But this Yearbook did not even bother to compare the Nazi elections with one another. Perhaps the Nazis missed a propaganda chance here; for it is quite an accomplishment to increase a party's vote from 43.9% of the total to 95.3% in the course of a few months, as did the Nazis between March and November, 1933. Of course, the percentage for the Fuehrer dropped back to 89.9% in August, 1934, but they soon got it up again. In 1936, 99.5% of all qualified voters did their duty, and 98.8% did it right by casting ballots "For the List and for the Fuehrer." There were by now so few negative votes that the statistical office simply lumped them together with the invalid ballots. After the great success in getting an expression of the people's will to follow the leader in 1936, there was no new plebiscite until the empire had expanded to take in more of the German folk. In April, 1938, the Austrians were allowed to show how devoted they were to the Fuehrer and how glad to be absorbed by the New State. The Sudeten Germans were given the same privilege in due time. After that there were no plebiscites. The war was on. But in the reporting of 1938 elections in the 1939 Yearbook a slight change was made. What had been called Austria in 1938 was now called "former Austria." One must remember that the German name for Austria means Eastern Empire, obviously not a fit name for a rather insignificant part of the all-inclusive eternal Greater German Empire.

Race in the pre-Nazi Yearbooks, was a characteristic of stallions. The number of their registered services for the propagation of their respective races was faithfully recorded in the agricultural part of the book. Men, on the other hand, had religion. They were Christians of Protestant or Roman-Catholic confession, or they were Israelites. That took in most Germans; a handful of others were lumped together. The 1932 book showed how many of each of these categories had lived in various parts and in the whole of Germany in 1910 and in 1925. The only other tables of religion are those which show the religion of each partner in all marriages of the previous year. Religion is indirectly shown in the tables of membership in trade unions and professional organizations, for some such organizations were Catholic or Protestant. None was specifically Jewish. In the first Hitler Yearbook, 1933, the references to religion are exactly as before—with one exception. The trade unions had already been dissolved. The book listed the divisions of the new Labor Front, but regretted that membership figures were not yet available. They were not in the next book, or the one after that, or ever. Perhaps, since all workers belonged to the Labor Front by definition, it would have been silly to give figures; they would have been the same as the figures of people employed in each occupation and industry.

The expressions Jew, Jewess, and Jewish do not occur in the pre-Nazi books or in the first Hitler Yearbook, 1933. Some people were of Israelite religion; some men and women of Israelite religion were married to women and men of the same religion or of Protestant, Roman Catholic or other faiths. That was all. The 1934 Yearbook reports a new religious Census made in 1933, and compares the religious composition of the population of that year with that of 1925. The 1910 comparison was dropped. The same words are still used for the various religions. But in 1935, although the same figures and the same words were used, there is a whole new set of tables which tell us all about some people called *Glaubensjuden,* of whom a special census had been taken on the 16th of June, 1933. They must be the same people who were formerly of Israelite religion, because there are exactly as many of them. But the change is more than one of name. The 1935 Yearbook picks these *Glaubensjuden* out for special attention not given people of other religions. We are shown what percent Jews form of the population in all geographic divisions; how many of them live in cities of more than 100,000, more than 50,000 and so on. The Jewish populations of Berlin, Hamburg, Frankfurt, Breslau and a few other large cities are shown in a separate table. The places of birth of Jews are tabulated, also the number and percent of them who are of German or foreign birth, and subjects of Germany or of other countries.

By this time, the Nuremberg laws had made a distinction between people who are subjects of Germany and those who are citizens. The Jews were subjects but could not be citizens. No such facts are presented for the population at large, or for Protestants or Catholics. It is clear that statistics on the Jews are of special interest to the government. We may fairly assume that the statistician had been told to prepare special data on Jews—and to change their names. The name *Glaubensjuden* (Jews by faith) is still one without racial connotation. Only in the tables on marriages and the religion of people who were born or who died in Prussia were there still people of Israelite religion. In fact, Israelites continued to be born, get married, and to die right down until 1939-40, while people called "Jews by faith" had occupations and lived in various places. In the 1939-40 Yearbook this name is dropped, and tables give us some new categories which take account of the finer distinctions of the Nuremberg laws: Jews, Jewish mixtures of the first degree and Jewish mixtures of the second degree in all parts of Germany, including Austria, for 1939. The same book still gives a table on the religion of the people, including Israelite. But in 1941-42, there is no longer an Israelite religion in German statistics. The religious categories are Protestant, Roman Catholic, Believers in God, and others. The *Gleichschaltung* of the statistics is complete. Jews are a race, not a religious group. German statistical segregation is also complete. Jews appear nowhere as simply another category of people in tables which include other Germans. There is one little exception: the good old Prussian vital statistics still show that people of Israelite religion are born and die. The Prussian civil servant is a stubborn fellow. He does his duty, come what may. Or maybe no one issued a new form for recording births and deaths in Prussia, and the officials just had to go on using the old ones.

Of all Israelite women married in 1930, one in eight married a Christian; of Israelite men, one in four married a Christian. From 1933 on, these proportions constantly decreased. In 1936, about one in fifty married out. The people of Germany were being *gleichgeschaltet;* but the statistical Yearbook stuck to its old form of reporting marriages by religion. Only in 1939-40 does racial reporting take the place of religious in marriage tables. There is in the book of that year a table showing the "Racial Classification of People Who Married in 1938." Marriage partners are now of five kinds: German-blooded, Jewish mixtures of the first degree, Jewish mixtures of the second degree, Jews and Jewesses, and persons of other foreign blood. Twenty-five German-blooded men married Jewesses, and thirty-three Jewish men married German-blooded women in that year. But these traitors to German blood were nearly all of foreign nationality; in 1939, no German-blooded subject of the Reich married a Jew or Jewess. *Gleichschaltung* both of marriage and marriage statistics was complete.

The Reich statistician was prodded, I suspect, into setting up tables and graphs to show at a glance the progress of the New State's program of prosperity and territorial expansion. He never showed in a summary and graphic way the success of the program to rid the country and the folk of foreign (Jewish) blood. One has to dig the facts out from many tables. In 1910 there were 538,909 people of Israelite religion in the Reich; 564,379 in 1925; 499,682 in 1933. One can also figure it out that in 1939 there were 451,451 of the people called Jews, Jewish mixtures of the first degree and Jewish mixtures of the second degree in the new Greater Germany. The Nazi regime could have taken credit for most of the decrease of Jewish people between 1925 and 1933, and certainly they could claim as their own the whole decrease of 48,000 between 1933 and 1939. They could have made their success more impressive by reminding the reader that the new Germany of 1939 included new eastern territory in which many Jews had lived. They could have shown in a more prominent place the reduction in percentage of Jewish population. In 1910 and 1925 nearly one German in a hundred had been a Jew; in 1939, only about one in 190. The Yearbook could also have made a better story out of emigration. It reported only those emigrants who went overseas, and failed to tell how many of them were Jews rather than people of true German blood. This was corrected in later books; for the years 1937, 1938, and 1939 Jewish overseas emigrants are shown separately from others. Until then the total number of overseas emigrants per year had remained between 12,000 and 15,000 since before the Nazi time. Emigration overseas was 14,203 in 1937; 22,986 in 1938; 25,818 in 1939. One can see in a separate table that 7,155 of the emigrants in 1937 were Jews; 16,561 in 1938, and 22,706 in 1939. The reader has to figure out for himself that while in 1937 only half the emigrants were Jews, over 90% of them were Jews in 1939. In still another table, the reader could learn that true Germans were actually coming home from overseas in greater number than they were leaving. In 1939, only 3,112 people not of Jewish blood emigrated overseas, while 10,455 came back to live or die under the New Order. The statistician could have put these things all together so that a person could follow with pride the purifying of his folk. But no; he reported it only bit by bit, grudgingly.

He did a little better for Prussia. Prussia, in its old-fashioned way, kept right on reporting births and deaths by religion, and persisted in considering that there was an Israelite religion—a fallacy that the New State had given up. If this kind of reporting had been done for all of Germany, one could have had an ideal record of the progress of the liquidation of

the Jews. As it is, we do know from various tables that there
were 370,348 Prussian Israelites in 1910; 404,446 in 1925;
361,826 Prussian Jews by faith in 1933; and 233,727 Jews,
Jewish mixtures of the first and second degrees in the larger
Prussia in 1939. Some measure of success is seen in the fact
that actually one person in a hundred was a Jew in 1925 in
Prussia, but only about half a person in a hundred in 1939.
But how was the success achieved? Through encouraging
emigration and the death rate? Or by discouraging the birth
rate? One has to work hard to get some idea of the weights
of these various methods. By using a lot of tables and making
some assumptions of the kind that statisticians make, one
can estimate that about 42,000 Prussian Jews emigrated overseas from 1933 to the end of August, 1939. As to the births,
2,100 children were born to Jewish mothers in Prussia in
1933, and about 100 to other mothers but of Jewish fathers.
The births decreased steadily until 1939, when only 478 were
born to Jewish mothers and less than fifty to other mothers
and Jewish fathers. This was a good solid reduction of 75%
in the number of Jews being produced by birth. But that is
a slow method of liquidation. It depends too much upon the
life-span. In the meantime, in spite of the smaller number of
Jews left in Prussia, the death figure held up very well. In
1933, when there were 361,826 Jews in Prussia, 5,565 died.
The number of deaths remained above 5,000 a year right
along. In 1938, for instance, 5,632 died.

In 1939 the number of deaths weakened a little to 5,182.
But since there were then only 233,727 Jews and mixtures
left in Prussia, the death rate was more than holding its own.
Just think of it: the Jewish population was down 128,099
in six years, a good 35%, without making a dent in the
number of Jews who died every year! A pretty good record,
all in all, when one remembers that the big campaign had not
really started yet. But the statistician should have saved the
reader all this trouble. He should have coordinated his statis-

tics about this program of the New State, just as for others. I begin to think he wasn't really *gleichgeschaltet* at all. It is too late for him to make it good now. The 1941-42 Yearbook was the eighth and last put out by the 1,000-Year Reich.

To be sure, a new series of Yearbooks has been started. The first is out: Statistical Yearbook of the German Federal Republic, 1952. It looks a lot like the old ones. The Foreword, signed by one Dr. Gerhard Fuerst, is short and businesslike. He tells of the technical difficulties caused by loss of records and by changes in boundaries. A lot of the tables are devoted to the many refugees from the east. The New State of the Nazis, like the new eastern-zone Democratic German Republic, exported refugees. The new western Federal Republic of Germany receives refugees.

The new western statistical German has lost his race and got back his religion. Some of them even belong to "the Jewish religious community." Not many; just 17,116 as compared with 103,293 in the same territory in 1939. I am glad to say that the new statistician doesn't even try to tell us what happened to the others. I wish him well, and hope he will never have to face the problems of his immediate predecessors.

13

Professional and Career Problems
of Sociology

SOCIOLOGY, being itself a social phenomenon, may be studied as one. One might try to find out, for instance, what the circumstances are under which people want to study human society in the way called sociological, those under which they are allowed to do so, and those under which they may publish and otherwise use their findings. Our discussion of the training and professional activities assumes some freedom in these matters. We have before us questions of narrower range, but nonetheless of great practical importance; questions about the organization of sociological activity. For my remarks on some of these problems I take as my cue the term *profession.*

Profession has in English a rather more special meaning than has the same word in French and its counterpart, *Beruf,* in German. A profession is an occupation which has attained a special standing among occupations. In the Western world, and more so in the English-speaking part of it, many occupations have sought this status in recent decades. At the same time a great many new subdivisions of learning and scientific

Transactions of the Second World Congress of Sociology. Vol. I, 1954. Pp. 178-85.

investigation have arisen. The people who have founded and/or pursue these new branches have also sought for their subjects and for themselves a place in the academic and scientific world like that of other, older branches, but separate from them. So numerous are these new occupations and branches of learning that one may compare the steps they take to achieve their end of attaining professional status, and thus arrive at a general description of the process of professionalizing an occupation. Against such a background one may see with more detachment and perhaps with more penetrating vision the situation and problems of organized sociology.

The first people to practise a new line of work come into it from other occupations. Youngsters do not ordinarily establish new occupations; it is done by more mature people who see a new need or a new opportunity. Sometimes they slip over into a new activity without thinking of it as an occupation, and are only later aware of the significance of the change. In other cases they are apostles, full of enthusiasm and charism, spreading the light of new knowledge and a new cause.

At some point these irregulars, having become aware of themselves as a new group with a social identity, set about setting the terms of entry of their successors, the second generation. Almost invariably they seek to straighten the career line. They set up devices to require their successors to choose the occupation earlier, to make them follow a set course of study and training, to enter into the work as a sole and continued way of making a living, and to do the work under institutional arrangements defined and enforced by the members of the occupation. On the social psychological side they insist that the individual accept identification with the occupation as part of his definition of himself, as a significant and persistent answer to the self-put question, "Who am I?" and the question put by others, "Who are you?" The true members of the aspiring profession will be thought to be those who enter it early, get the conventional training, work at the trade, identify themselves with its collective activities, and leave it only when they leave off working altogether. A person who, once in the charmed circle, leaves it, thereby slights the profession as a whole. He makes light of dedication to it and calls down upon himself that anger which reaches its extreme in the attitude toward a priest who gives up the cloth. The professional group seeks to become an enduring thing in two senses; first, in that membership in it should be enduring and, second, in that the group itself lasts as a known and accepted organ of society.

In this latter aspect, the professional group will claim the mandate to select, train, initiate and discipline its own members and to define the nature of the services which they will perform and the terms on which they will perform them. If possible, they will extend this mandate to the point of monopoly, excluding others from performing their kind of work, and seeking the exclusive prerogative of defining the proper relations (ethic) between the professionals and all other people concerned in their work. In its full form, the mandate will include the function of developing a philosophy for society at large concerning the whole area of thought, value and action involved directly or even remotely in their work. How far these mandates will be realized depends upon many circumstances, including competition and conflicts with other occupations and interests.

The course of a new branch of learning is rather like that of a new occupation which, indeed, it tends to become. Part of its course will depend upon how much it becomes involved in the giving of services to individual clients, or to institutions or the public as collective clients. If it is closely related to a service it will seek to follow the model of a profession, as just outlined. If it gives no immediate service it may follow the model of older so-called pure sciences. In this case the group may not strive so hard to close its ranks or to seek a monopoly from society. In America the psychologists are in a conflict as to whether psychology will be primarily a science or primarily a profession. I do not suggest that they have a choice. The logic of circumstances will almost certainly require them as a group to be both, although some individuals may be purely scientific experimenters while others are therapists. I suspect it is the fate of sociology to suffer a similar chronic conflict. It may not be so acute, as sociology is not likely to be used as an instrument of individual therapy to such an extent as psychology. But if our problem of defining professional relations with individual clients is less acute, our relations with institutions, the state and society are likely to be more trying. Although many sociologists would like to consider their work politically neutral, it is not considered so by those who make revolutions of right or left, or by those who have special interests in the things we study. However strongly we may emulate the model of pure science, claims for applying our knowledge and the fact that what we learn is never a matter of social indifference will continue to put us into the position of people who give a service (or do a disservice) to our client, society. We cannot decide once and for all to be completely a profession or completely a science. The problem is chronic, as are all the basic problems with which professional groups have to deal. The basic parts of any professional code concerns such problems, those which cannot be settled once and for all, but for which—within the limits of lasting principles—different solutions have to be found according to the circumstances of time and place. We should, as an international society, be very chary of trying to determine in any detail solutions to apply to all of the many countries and situations in which sociologists have to work.

In America, at least, we have already gone far upon the road of professionalizing our occupation in one respect. We are pushing the point of crucial decision to enter upon sociological study back to an ever earlier point in the schooling, hence in the life, of the individual. This is justified by the contention that, as our methods develop, the prerequisite knowledge and skills become greater. With more to be learned, if the age of completing training remain the same, the starting point must be earlier. This argument is hard to answer. One must, however, take care to distinguish between conventional and strictly necessary prerequisite training. It is very easy to let prerequisites degenerate into a device to enforce early choice and to ensure proper indoctrination of potential members of an occupation or academic branch. Great is the temptation to raise the status of our subject by proving that it takes as long to become a sociologist as to become a physicist or physician. The best proof is simple; one makes it a rule. I doubt very much whether we know the best possible prerequisite training for sociologists. And since we are still a new and exploring subject we probably should not harden our programme of training too much lest we thereby also harden our subject and methods.

Furthermore, we do not know what effect early choice of sociology as a field of professional study will have upon the kinds of persons who will elect the field. It may be early choice would draw in people of some one bent, with a tendency toward selecting for study only those problems and toward using only those methods which fit the concept of sociology crystallized in the conventional prerequisites. Students entering medical schools show a tendency to pick those specialties which are well known and which are vaunted by their teachers as embodying the true model of medical practice. Choice of others, such as psychiatry, psychosomatic medicine, epidemiology and public health, often comes quite late and after some ripening experience in which the young man, in effect, unlearns some things and sets out upon a new and less well-charted course of new learning. If we set the point of crucial decision to enter sociology too early, we may prevent that later change of interest which has given us so many of the best sociologists. For sociology is analogous, in this regard, not to a profession, but to a specialty within the larger profession of studying human affairs. If we apply rigid rules of entry to training, we may limit too much the circulation of people, hence of minds, from one branch of social science to another. Since ours is still one of the less known branches, we stand to gain from second and third choices. Furthermore, it may well be that interest in scientific analysis of societies in sociological terms is a mature one, a by-product of other training and experience. Our problem is to develop devices for training people to a high level of theoretical and technical competence without too much restriction of circulation from one branch of social science and experience to another, and without forcing the choice to a too early age.

There is a problem of circulation of sociologists later in their careers as well as during their training. An occupation in course of becoming a profession (and a new branch of learning in course of finding its place) will strive to solve the related problems of circulation and careers in two dimensions at the same time. On the one hand they will seek to set up strong and clear boundaries between their occupation and all others, and to develop career opportunities for those within. On the other hand, they will complement this clear bounding with an attempt to make the profession more universal, so that the professional may carry on his work in a greater variety of situations; so that his skill may meet the needs of any client whatsoever or so that his methods of investigation (in the case of a science) may be applied anywhere and at any time with equal validity. In the purest case the professional would do work which he alone can do, and the work would be of a kind wanted everywhere by all men; a maximum of specific bounding would be matched by a maximum of universality. Armed with his special qualifications, the ideal professional could go from job to job, client to client, place to place, and from country to country; so could the pure scientist. I suppose the best living model of this is the profession of medicine. Physicians have come as close as one can easily imagine to excluding all others from practise of their profession. They also perform a service that may be conceived as universal in character and as universally wanted. Actually, even in this case the reality does not completely correspond to the model. The boundaries between physical illness and spiritual illness are not clear and the definitions of illness and health vary from society to society. Sick people may want a doctor of their own kind, and not willingly accept strangers. Other people than physicians also share the treatment of people's troubles. Furthermore, the doctor's knowledge and skills are not completely universal. Some of them refer to the illnesses endemic in his own country. Finally, doctors in one country or place will not willingly allow strangers to come among them and compete for clients. So that, even this most specific and universal of professions does not achieve full monopoly as against other occupations and does not allow completely free circulation of professionals from place to place and situation to situation. The case of medicine shows that even in the extreme case the solutions are relative, not absolute. How sharply should and can sociologists in fact be set off as a peculiar group with specific careers reserved to them alone? How universal can their knowledge and skills of investigation be made? Consequently, in how large an area may they move around freely in course of their careers? I will discuss the last question first, and then return to the other one.

Of recent years there has been a healthy moving around of sociologists. We have met one another, held such meetings as this, worked in one another's universities and institutes. In some countries we have profited from the forced migration of sociologists from other countries. Perhaps we are closer to developing a universal conception of sociological study than ever before. On the other hand it is likely that most sociological careers will be confined to one country. Some sociologists will circulate in two or three closely related countries. A very few will move about in a really wide space. More will visit other countries for varying lengths of time. While the theoretical systems and the basic techniques for studying society should be universal, most sociologists get familiar with the historic conditions of one or two countries, with certain specific problems or institutions and with certain social changes in the setting of their own country or region. The methods may be universal; the data to which they are applied are historical.

In one sense a sociologist—as Robert E. Park used to say—tells the news, although in a more exact way and also in a more general and abstract way than do newspapers. It is not likely that we will ever be free of the demand that we show special interest in and knowledge of the conditions and changes in the world around us. For one thing observation of the human data on which we base our theoretical analysis depends generally on fairly intimate contact with persons and institutions. While playing the role of the timeless and disinterested outsider is an important item in the repertoire of the social scientist, it is not the whole of it. Our role requires also intense curiosity and personal concern about the people and problems studied. I predict that for these reasons, and for the more embarrassing one that even sociologists may be slightly ethnocentric and perhaps even concerned about foreign competition, most sociological careers will be played out within national boundaries.

Then comes the question of the possibility of having careers within countries, or regions of two or more countries which make up effective circulating areas. The possibilities obviously depend both upon the institutional organization of academic and scientific activities within a given country and upon the size of the area. America, north of the Mexican border, forms a vast area with essentially the same institutional forms and with a great demand for people who go by the name of sociologist. The career possibilities are great. A young man may be fairly sure that he may choose from among a number of open places when he finishes his training, and that he may from there on move about from position to position to suit his talents and his special interests. If he does not succeed in getting a position where he may do specialized research, or if he does not wish to do so he can become one of the army of college teachers. College teaching absorbs many who are called, but not quite chosen. The number of positions in better known universities, in research organizations and in agencies which want people who can apply sociological knowledge are themselves numerous enough so that no competently trained and talented sociologist need want for a choice of jobs. In these circumstances there is ample opportunity for circulating careers within a fairly closely defined profession of sociologists (although it is still questionable how closely the professional group should be defined).

Many of our ideas concerning the professionalizing of an academic subject rest upon the assumption of such a large market. But the academic market for all subjects is small in many countries and especially so for a new subject such as sociology. Generally speaking, there is no great absorbing institution for sociologists in other countries as in the United States and Canada. The sociologist cannot be absorbed by the European Gymnasium or Lycée as easily as by the American college. One of the problems of a new and fairly specialized subject in a small country is precisely the possibility of absorbing those who study the subject, but who do not immediately—if ever—enter upon the main career line in which the training would be used. In French Canada, for instance, there are three universities. Sociology is new in them. Once the few positions are filled there will not be places for an annual crop of talented young men trained as specialists in sociology. But without an annual crop of talented young people the subject itself languishes. Without a position in which he can use his knowledge and skill the young man languishes; or he finds another kind of place, and his skill languishes. The problem might be solved by increasing the area in which the individual may circulate in course of his career. We have already raised that question. It might also be solved by combining sociology with other activities, which means some departure from the ideal of complete professional specialization. For the model of complete specialization implies a large market. Even in the large market, it is not completely realized in many occupations. Nor is it at all certain that it is the most efficient model for all kinds of activities. Research has never been fully separated from teaching in most academic subjects; in spite of all that has been said there is not the slightest evidence that it would be wise to do so. Few professions have ever achieved such specialization that the practitioner carries on only one activity. The lawyer writes a brief, but he also pleads and arbitrates. Priests preach, hear confessions and administer the affairs of the Church. Physicians diagnose, treat, and investigate. The historic connection of teaching and research may be weakened in some fields, and certainly the best balance between them is not the same in all. But even where research stands alone as a professional activity, new people must be taught to carry it on. The connection is inescapable, although the weighting of the two activities in a given man's career may vary. There can also be other connections; as for instance, combinations of sociological research with practical activities of various kinds. We who are in the larger countries should be cautious in promoting concepts of professional specialization which do not suit conditions in other countries. (I think I can assume that we are all more interested in the advancement of sociological knowledge than in the advancement of a profession of sociology.)

Specialization and the closed profession should be instruments, not ends in themselves. It may well be that sociology will have to be combined with other activities in many countries if there is to be that amount of circulation which will keep new recruits coming into it, and which will make for a large enough group of collaborators to stimulate one another and to get the work of sociological analysis of the life of the country done.

The combination of sociology with other things that comes most easily to mind is that with other branches of social science and with the various kinds of social practice. And here we are back again with our problem of setting the boundaries of sociology, or rather, of the group of people called sociologists. The questions for solution are still both theoretical and practical. We may ask what combinations of sociology with other social or other sciences are best for the advancement of knowledge about man and society. This includes the basic question about what the effective divisions of social science will be in the future; we all know that the divisions of physical and biological science are not what they once were. The practical question—itself not free of theoretical aspects—is that of the best institutional organisation, including that of the best degree of separation of the sociological career from others. All will probably agree that a subject will not advance well unless there are nuclei of people in a position to give their undivided attention to it, nor will it flourish without that morale which comes of being a member of a group with a strong sense of colleagueship and a clear sense of common task. The developing and strengthening of such nuclei is certainly a major problem for sociologists in many countries. Their efforts to create more chairs of sociology, and to get more general recognition of the subject and more money for teaching and research will certainly be supported with enthusiasm by all of us. But I think it likely that these nuclei will function more effectively if the boundaries between us and related social sciences are not drawn too closely. Of course it is sometimes true that those closest to us are our bitterest opponents; nor am I unaware of the fact that economists and historians have sometimes effectively hindered the development of sociology by teaching a little of it themselves and pretending that no more is necessary (just as in the U. S. a university will hire one Negro professor to prove that it doesn't discriminate against Negroes). These dangers, like others, are chronic. I still believe that the best formula for sociology is to develop strong working nuclei of people, without drawing the boundaries too tightly between ourselves and our colleagues in other branches of social science and social practice. Circulation from one branch to another should be easy, so far as institutional and professional barriers are concerned; difficult in the sense that we set high standards of competence for ourselves, our collaborators and our apprentices. Sociology began as the maverick of the social sciences. Bastard child of philosophy, her fatherhood sometimes claimed, sometimes rejected by history, sibling or cousin of economics, political science, anthropology and psychology, let her stand on the privilege of her unique parentage by not following too closely the model of an exclusive profession.

Postscript

Two Worlds:

Social Science and the Cosmos

First Scene

[Characters:

Little Boy, with a full, cherubic, but impassive face; in fact, a dead pan. Speaks in a persistent monotone, dead serious. Often breaks in when papa speaks, but without any sense of interrupting. He is just talking on in his God-driven way. No facial reaction; no gestures. In fact, I think he may be a professor dressed up as a little boy.

Papa, a big, important looking papa.

Papa discovered in his library, or his office; take your pick. He sits at a desk cluttered with papers. He is a busy man. He works at home, drawing up papers for new companies and foundations and things. Why is his desk cluttered, and he an important man? His wife won't let him bring his secretary home, that's why.

Little Boy stands by desk with a toy engine in his hand.]

Little Boy: Papa, buy me a new train.

Papa: Why son, surely the train Santa Claus brought you on Christmas is still new and perfectly good. (Reader, You're wrong. The little boy does not look pityingly at papa for his faith in Santa Claus. This is no ordinary smart-alec modern child.)

Why, when I was a little boy I thought I was lucky. . . .

BOY: (*Interrupting*) I need a new train.

PAPA: Now why on earth do you *need* a new train?

BOY: I am going to make some scientific experiments.

PAPA: (*Getting a proud papa glint in his eye*) Why, that's wonderful. Scientific experiments! (*Dreamy-eyed*) Scientific experiments! I always wanted to be a scientist—busting atoms, dissolving moons, making star dust, crumbling earth. (*Hauling himself together*) But money, money! Making money got me, and deprived me of my youth. Well, well, son, you can rise on the back of your poor father. But, seriously now, since you are interested in electricity, isn't there other equipment better than a train for making experiments?

BOY: I am not interested in electricity. I need a train.

PAPA: (*Disappointed*) But you said you wanted to make experiments. Now there isn't any other kind of train except electric. Of course, in my day there were those old-fashioned key-winders. . . .

BOY: (*Cutting in, but dead pan and deliberate*) Papa, there are lots of kinds of trains. Steam, diesel, and soon there will be jet and atomic-powered locomotion.

PAPA: Oh, yes, son, of course, of course, I know that, but we are talking about *toy* trains. Now. . . .

BOY: I am not talking about toy trains.

PAPA: Look here, son, this has gone far enough. Go back to your play room and let me alone. I have work to do.

BOY: But, papa, I have to make some experiments to find out how fast you can run a train without it flying to pieces. I need a train that runs from here to St. Louis with lots of people in it. I will probably need another one next week, too.

(*Papa nearly faints, but takes a second look at the dead pan of his wonder boy and, hypnotized, picks up the phone.*)

PAPA: (*into phone*) Miss Indispensable? Get Dick Smith,

President of the Smoky Valley Railroad on the phone. Yes,
I know it is after dinner in the evening. But, say, (*taking another look at the boy*), don't bother about the phone; go to
his home and fetch him over here right away.

(*Fast Curtain*)

Second Scene

[Characters:

Same boy, dressed up as a modern professor. Good haircut,
shoes shined and everything. What color of suit and tie? You
don't catch me there; he is so well dressed you wouldn't be able
to tell. You wouldn't notice, even. *He* married *his* secretary.

Same papa, now dressed up as Foundation official. Both are
longer winded than before.

Scene is the same, too, except for the portrait of an old party
on the wall. A caption says this old party is Sylvester Makestuff,
Foundryman and Founder.

The desk is all clear except for one neatly bound manuscript
all tied up with a ribbon.

Both papa and boy—I mean, professor—discovered as before.
Since he is dressed up as a professor, the boy is seated on a
chair across the desk from the man. He has no toy engine in his
hand; or has he? Suppose I just go on calling them Papa and Boy.]

PAPA: Now would you kindly explain to me a little further
the nature of the experiments you would like to make and
give me an estimate of what they would cost. You see, reading
tires me (*lifts ribboned manuscript and drops it, showing
that ribbon has not been untied. Ah, this is the precious re-*

search proposal and request for money that the Boy's—I mean Professor's—secretary sat up nights typing all last month.) In fact, my doctor has warned me against reading in any way, shape or form. And as for figures. . . . After all, we do have television these days, don't we? By the way, would you like to see my set? (*Warming to the subject*) It's a Superduper Nth Power. I was just watching Gorgeous Georgia when you came in. That's why I kept you waiting. Ha, Ha, Ha. Hope you didn't mind. I bet you wonder where the set is. Well, it's behind that third panel on the opposite wall. I just push a button and there it is. Don't even have to turn my head. You would never have guessed it was there, would you, now? Ha, ha, ha. You see, whoever sits where you are has his back to it and doesn't. . . .

BOY: I will need about half a billion to start.

PAPA: (*Awakened from his TV reverie to the smooth and shining nightmare in front of him*) Half a billion to start? Huh, what's that? Oh yes, where were we? (*Collecting himself and assuming an impassive expression himself*) Now what university did you say you were from? Ha, ha, ha, silly question, isn't it? What difference does it make? But I have to ask, you know. The Board members insist on it. They like to play games to keep them awake at meetings—sticking pins in a map to show where their money goes! Ha, ha—not that it's really their money, you know, ha, ha, ha, but they like to make believe. . . .

BOY: (*Interrupting*) Of course, the half billion is only a starter. It won't last long. I will use a quarter billion to develop our experimental designs and to build equipment for trial runs. Then a second quarter billion will go for retooling our psychotrone and Polterkammer for the first real experiments on how to run the world.

PAPA: (*Whose hand was restlessly feeling around for his television button, but suddenly was arrested by the look in the boy's eyes*) Half a billion just for the trial experiments? You did say half a billion, didn't you? Never mind what university you came from. I'm glad you came. It gets so dull here in the office most days. Between you and me this job bores me stiff. Everybody so serious. Some nights my wife has to massage my face for two hours before she gets it loosened up enough so she can tell by my expression whether I am lying or not when I say I had to stay late in the office. Sometimes she has to smack my face to break the crust on it. You know, sitting here all day listening to all that stuff about research to save the world without looking either interested or uninterested. But you're different. You're fun. Go on, tell me more about the ten billions—it was ten billions, wasn't it? And about how you are going to run the world!

BOY: You wouldn't understand the experiment, really. It is scientific. Of course, we will put it into simple graphic form for television later on. You can see it then. I aim to develop a set of encyclopedic tables for human behavior; you know—like the periodic tables in chemistry. We're just a new science, but we are ready for that phase now. We're about twenty years behind nuclear physics, but that is good. They need that much start so as to be useful to us five years from now. In fact, we will probably have to show them how to train people so they can develop their science fast enough to keep up with us.

PAPA: But what do you need now?

BOY: Now? In simple language for you and your Board, we need a Supreme Court to experiment with. It will be expensive; a building like the present one, but with lots of secret electronic equipment, gasonometers, lietesters, forgetometers, boastographs, pomposodetectors, etc. We'll use much more eavesdropping equipment than the FBI. Oh, yes, we will need some Judges, too—they come high sometimes.

PAPA: Oh, I see, you want to hire some students to act

just like Supreme Court Judges. And then you would offer them money and find out their price. You would use students instead of rats! Ha, ha, ha.

BOY: No, we will use real Supreme Court Judges. There is a great deal to be learned about rat behavior in that way. We thought of using deans, but we couldn't get a good control group of rats—I mean, humans just like deans in every way except that they would not be deans. The demand for deans is too great. But it is easy to match Supreme Court Judges; lots more candidates than places. You can get a control group easy if you have the money. So you can tell whether they're like that anyway, or whether it is because they are judges.

PAPA: So you would set up a fake—I mean, an *experimental* Supreme Court and pretend to have cases tried, and you would be behind the wall pushing buttons and turning lights on and off to confuse the judges. How very original! But still, 20 billion is a lot of money, even for a fake court.

BOY: I mean a *real* Supreme Court—*The* Supreme Court, with real cases. We could learn a lot about the legal mind that way. We always start with the simplest case in science. Then we extrapolate our knowledge to more complicated minds.

PAPA: You mean the real Court with real Judges and real cases sent up by real people?

BOY: (*Remember he is insistently impassive*) That would be just the first experiment. Of course, eventually we will have to depend upon astronomy.

PAPA: Astronomy? Is that a behavioral science now, too?

BOY: Well, if we are to learn how to run this world we need another identical with it to experiment on. Maybe two, or three, in case we blow up one or two. According to the laws of chance, there must be several planets in the universe just like Earth down to the last rat. If the astronomers would only realize how little time there is and get out and find at least one of those twins of Earth, we could learn how to run a world. Hard to work fast with only one guinea pig.

PAPA: (*Hypnotized again. Reaches for a huge check book and pen*) Well, well, this has been a great day. My face is as soft and relaxed as a baby's. Hope my wife won't ask me where I was last night. Astronomic, I call it. Positively astronomic. By the way, son, which world are you going to experiment on, Earth or that other one the astronomers are going to find for you? I have to move in the spring.

(*Curtain*)

Bibliography

Asheim, Lester (ed.) *A Forum on the Public Library Inquiry.*
New York, 1950.

Barrett, E. Boyd. *Ex-Jesuit.* London, 1930.

Becker, Howard S. "The Professional Dance Musician and his
Audience," *The American Journal of Sociology,* Vol. LVII
(September, 1951), pp. 136-44.

Bladen, V. W. "Economics and Human Relations," *The Canadian
Journal of Economics and Political Science,* Vol. 14 (August,
1948), pp. 301-11.

Bulletin of the American Association of University Professors.
Vol. XXI (March, 1935), "The University of Pittsburgh,"
pp. 224-66. Vol. XIX (November, 1933), "Rollins College,"
pp. 416-38.

Carr-Saunders, A.M., and Wilson, P. A. *The Professions.*
Oxford, 1933.

Catholic Encyclopedia, Vol. XV, "Vocation."

Cooley, C. H. *Social Organization.* New York, 1909.

Defoe, Daniel. *The True-Born Englishman.*

Dix, Gregory. *The Shape of the Liturgy.* London, 1947.

Donovan, Frances R. *The Woman Who Waits.* Boston, 1920.

Durkheim, Emile. *De la division du travail social.* 2e édition.
Paris, 1902.

Faris, E. "The Primary Group: Essence and Accident," *The
American Journal of Sociology,* Vol. XXXVIII (July, 1932),
pp. 41-50.

Fenichel, O. *Hysterien und Zwangsneurosen.* Vienna, 1931.

Field, Mark G. "Structured Strain in the Role of the Soviet
Physician," *The American Journal of Sociology,* Vol. LVIII
(March, 1953), pp. 493-502.

Gold, Ray. "Janitors vs. Tenants: a Status-income Dilemma,"

The American Journal of Sociology, Vol. LVII (March, 1952), pp. 487-93.

Goldsmith, Oliver. *Essay on Education.*

Gennep, Arnold van. *Les rites de passage.* Paris, 1909

Gosse, Edmond. *Father and Son.* New York, 1907.

Hall, Oswald. *The Informal Organization of Medical Practice.* Unpublished Ph.D. dissertation, University of Chicago, 1944.

———. "The Stages of a Medical Career," *The American Journal of Sociology,* Vol. LIII (March, 1948), pp. 327-36.

Henderson, L. J. "Physician and Patient as a Social System," *The New England Journal of Medicine,* Vol. 212 (November, 1937), pp. 404-13.

Hughes, Everett C. *Cycles and Turning Points. A Faculty Paper.* New York, National Council of the Episcopal Church, 1952. Pp. 1-15.

———. "Dilemmas and Contradictions of Status," *The American Journal of Sociology,* Vol. L (March, 1945), pp. 353-59.

———. "Discussion of the Bryan Report," in Asheim, L. (Ed.) *A Forum on the Public Library Inquiry.* New York, 1950, pp. 106-14.

———. "The *Gleichschaltung* of the German Statistical Yearbook," *The American Statistician,* Vol. IX (December, 1955), pp. 8-11.

———. "Institutional Office and the Person," *The American Journal of Sociology,* Vol. XLIII (November, 1937), pp. 404-13.

———. "The Making of a Physician," *Human Organization,* Vol. 14 (Winter, 1955), pp. 21-25.

———. "Mistakes at Work," *The Canadian Journal of Economics and Political Science,* Vol. XVII (August, 1951), pp. 320-27.

———. "Personality Types and the Division of Labor," *The American Journal of Sociology,* Vol. XXXIII (March, 1928), pp. 754-68.

———. "Professional and Career Problems of Sociology," *Transactions of the Second World Congress of Sociology,* London, 1954. Vol. I, pp. 178-85.

————. "Psychology: Science and/or Profession," *The American Psychologist,* Vol. 7 (August, 1952), pp. 441-43.

————. "Social Role and the Division of Labor," *Bulletin of the Committee on Human Development,* University of Chicago, 1955, pp. 32-38. Also in *The Midwest Sociologist,* Vol. XVII (Spring, 1956), pp. 3-7.

————. "Work and the Self," in Rohrer, John H., and Sherif, M. (eds.), *Social Psychology at the Crossroads.* New York, 1951, pp. 313-23.

Hughes, Helen MacGill. "The Compleat Anti-Vivisectionist," *The Scientific Monthly,* Vol. LXV (December, 1947), pp. 503-07.

Johnson, James Weldon. *Along this Way.* New York, 1933.

Joshi, G. N., and Wadia, P. A. *Money and the Money Market in India.* London, 1926.

Kennedy, A. J., Farra, K., and associates. *Social Settlements in New York.* New York, 1935.

Klein, Melanie. "The Role of the School in the Libidinal Development of the Child," *International Journal of Psychoanalysis,* Vol. V (July, 1924), pp. 312-31.

Lasswell, H. D. *World Politics and Personal Insecurity.* New York, 1935.

Locke, John. *Letters concerning Toleration.* London, 1759.

Linton, Ralph. *The Study of Man.* New York, 1936.

McKenzie, R. D. "The Concept of Dominance and World Organization," *The American Journal of Sociology,* Vol. XXXIII (July, 1927), pp. 28-42.

Malinowski, B. *Argonauts of the Western Pacific.* London, 1922.

————. *Crime and Custom in Savage Society.* London, 1926.

Mannheim, Karl. "Ueber das Wesen und die Bedeutung des wirtschaftlichen Erfolgsstrebens," *Archiv fuer Sozialwissenschaft und Sozialpolitik,* Vol. 63 (June, 1930), pp. 449-512.

Marshall, T. H. "The Recent History of Professionalism in Relation to Social Structure and Social Policy," *The Canadian Journal of Economics and Political Science,* Vol. V (August, 1939), pp. 325-34.

Mayo, Elton W. *The Human Problems of an Industrial Civilization.* New York, 1933.

North, C. C. *Social Differentiation*. Chapel Hill, 1926.

Park, Robert E. "Human Migration and the Marginal Man," *The American Journal of Sociology*, Vol. XXXIII (May, 1928), pp. 881-93. Also in his *Race and Culture*. Glencoe, 1950.

Piaget, J. *The Moral Judgment of the Child*. London, 1932.

Redfield, R. *Chan Kom, a Maya Village*. Washington, 1934.

Riesman, David. "Toward an Anthropological Science of Law and the Legal Profession," *The American Journal of Sociology*, Vol. LVII (September, 1951), pp. 121-35.

Sigerist, Henry E. *A History of Medicine*. Vol. I. *Primitive and Archaic Medicine*. New York, 1951.

Smith, Adam. *The Wealth of Nations*.

Sombart, Werner. *Das Wirtschaftsleben im Zeitalter des Hochkapitalismus*. Munich, 1927.

Sorokin, P. *Social Mobility*. New York, 1927.

Sumner, W. G. *The Folkways*. Boston, 1906.

————. *War and Other Essays*. New Haven, 1911.

Tarbell, Ida M. *The Life of Elbert H. Gary*. New York, 1925.

Thomas, W. I. and Znaniecki, F. *The Polish Peasant in Europe and America*. New York, 1927.

Veblen, T. *The Higher Learning in America*. New York, 1918.

Webb, S. and B. *English Local Government; the Parish and the County*. London, 1900.

————. *A History of Trade Unionism*, rev. ed. London, 1920.

Weber, Max. *Gesammelte politische Schriften*. Munich, 1921.

————. *Gesammelte Aufsaetze zur Soziologie und Sozialpolitik*. Tuebingen, 1924.

White, Bouck. *The Book of Daniel Drew*. New York, 1910.

Whyte, William F. "Pity the Poor Personnel Man," *Advanced Management* (October-December, 1944), pp. 154-58.

Williams, Josephine J. "Patients and Prejudice," *The American Journal of Sociology*, Vol. LI (January, 1946), pp. 283-87.

Index

6936

DATE DUE